TODGER

TODGER

THOMAS JONES VC, DCM,

1ST BATTALION,
THE CHESHIRE REGIMENT

NEIL THORNTON

FONTHILL

Dedicated to Tony Bamber

Fonthill Media Language Policy

Fonthill Media publishes in the international English language market. One language edition is published worldwide. As there are minor differences in spelling and presentation, especially with regard to American English and British English, a policy is necessary to define which form of English to use. The Fonthill Policy is to use the form of English native to the author. Neil Thornton was born and educated Cheshire; therefore British English has been adopted in this publication.

Fonthill Media Limited
Fonthill Media LLC
www.fonthillmedia.com
office@fonthillmedia.com

First published in the United Kingdom and the United States of America 2021

British Library Cataloguing in Publication Data:
A catalogue record for this book is available from the British Library

ISBN 978-1-78155-787-7

Typeset in 10pt on 13pt Sabon
Printed and bound in England

Foreword

I have met two holders of the Victoria Cross in my lifetime. It was a singular honour and I was awestruck. Men who have won the VC are a very special band of brothers whose courage surpasses mortality. It is not that they are without fear—if so, there is no courage—but that they can overcome or hold that fear in check. Thomas Alfred Jones VC, DCM, known as 'Todger', was one such person—and what a person he was.

At the age of thirty-five, very old to be a front-line soldier in the Cheshire Regiment, Todger won the VC at the Battle of Morval on 25 September 1916. The exact details of how he did this are recorded in Chapter 6 of this excellent account of his life by author Neil Thornton. But even by the extraordinary bravery so often exhibited by others who won the VC, Todger's award stands out.

From the start of his personal attack on that day in 1916 until the end of this action, he was on his own, and that is extraordinary. For me, companionship in extreme danger is often a catalyst to courage—not wanting to let others down often gives wings to gallantry—but Todger deliberately set off from the relative safety of his front-line trench on his own. Despite being engaged by several snipers whose rounds hit his helmet and tunic, he dealt with each in turn and then forced the surrender of 102 Germans absolutely without any support from other soldiers. What an incredible action by this man from Runcorn.

Todger endured gas attacks during the Battle for Hill 60 and should have received a medal, but the officer making the recommendation was killed before doing the paperwork. On the Somme, Todger had to kill a Prussian Guard officer in hand-to-hand fighting. His letters home describe just how horrendous the conditions were for the soldiers. Indeed, he must have been one of the few front-line Cheshire soldiers that were serving near the beginning and at the end of the First World War, with so many of his comrades killed or severely wounded.

Throughout my own service with the Cheshires, every new young soldier joining the regiment was told about Todger Jones. He was and remains an inspiration to soldiers of our times too. Yet, as far as I know, Neil Thornton's book is the first comprehensive account of this extraordinarily gallant man, and it is not before time. I commend this book to anyone who wants to read about sheer guts and courage.

Bob Stewart
Col. (Ret'd) Bob Stewart DSO, MP
Commanding Officer
1st Battalion, 22nd (Cheshire) Regiment, 1991-93

Acknowledgements

My first acknowledgement must go to Bob Stewart DSO, MP, for providing the foreword for this publication. My gratitude extends to the Cheshire Regiment Museum in Chester and to Percy Dunbavand—my grandmother's cousin and the great-nephew of Todger Jones VC, DCM. Percy's first-hand memories, recollections, and family photos were of immense importance and hugely valuable to this book. The same applies to Anne Bamber, Todger's great-niece, whose knowledge and enthusiasm recounting family memories and allowing access to her extensive family archive was absolutely vital to this publication. Similarly, the information received from Paul Smitham, Todger's great-grandson, whose willingness to share stories from his side of the family, was very gladly received, as was Bill Raftery's recollections of watching Todger's graveside funeral service as a child.

My compliments extend to Graeme Ainsworth, who inadvertently provided me with the initial lead that helped finally identify Sam Poxon (Todger's best friend) after many unsuccessful years of trying, and to Richard Ault (*Stoke Sentinel*), for further information and images of 'Poggy'. Also, Mark Green (www.vconline.org), for helping with the location of sources and for supplying several photographs; Rob Clark, for his excellent service in fulfilling my research requests for those locations too distant to visit; and Liz Howard, for allowing me to use extracts from her research. Also, Stuart Allen and Peter Blackmore, both of whom assisted with local history; Kevin Brazier; and to Gary Tracey, who 'repaired' a badly damaged photograph of Todger that features in this publication. Lastly, thank you to my father, Eric Thornton, for his illustrations, and to Steve Noon for his painting of Todger that was commissioned especially for this book.

Contents

Introduction

'How the Dickens did you do it Jones?' asked King George as he presented Private T. A. Jones with his Victoria Cross at Buckingham Palace.[1]

It is perhaps difficult to comprehend how one man could accomplish what Pte Thomas 'Todger' Jones of the 1st Battalion, Cheshire Regiment, actually did to earn his VC. That a single individual, alone and unsupported in an enemy trench, could capture over 100 enemy soldiers may seem like an impossible feat, but that is exactly what Todger Jones succeeded in doing in September 1916 at Morval during the bloody Battle of the Somme. The remarkable circumstances surrounding his award mark it out as one of the most spectacularly earned in the history of that coveted award.

The VC was awarded 628 times in the First World War. This number does not include America's 'Unknown Soldier', or the five VCs awarded for actions against the Bolsheviks in Russia that followed the Armistice of the Great War, although these are sometimes included in the overall figure, depending on the source.

Two 'bars' are included in the number, each denoting a second award of the VC to an individual. Just three men have received a bar, two of which were awarded during the First World War.

Arthur Martin-Leake was the first to receive the VC and bar. As an officer in the Royal Army Medical Corps (RAMC), Martin-Leake's first award came as a result of his bravery in the Second Boer War in February 1902 when tending to wounded soldiers under a galling fire, which resulted in him receiving three bullet wounds.[2] Martin-Leake's bar was awarded in similar circumstances in the first months of the First World War, although on that occasion, he was fortunate enough to escape injury.

Capt. Noel Godfrey Chavasse was the second man to receive a bar during the war, and like Martin-Leake before him, he too belonged to the RAMC. Chavasse was a pre-war territorial attached to the Liverpool Scottish who had earned a

Military Cross for actions at Hooge in 1915. His VC was awarded the following year for his gallantry performed on 9 August 1916 at Guillemont on the Somme, and his bar for actions at Passchendaele in August 1917. Chavasse was mortally wounded during this action and subsequently passed away. His bar was the only one to be awarded posthumously.[3] As would be expected, all three of Chavasse's gallantry awards were for treating the wounded and for his complete disregard for his own safety while doing so.

The third recipient of the VC and bar was Capt. Charles Upham, a New Zealander who was awarded his distinctions at the sharp end of battle during the Second World War.

Todger Jones would find himself pitched into some of the Western Front's bloodiest actions. Miraculously, and despite numerous near-misses along the way, he would not only survive the war, but he would come through it without sustaining any serious wound.

Regarding his VC, it is doubtful that any individual British soldier surpassed the number of prisoners that Todger Jones secured single-handedly during the act for which it was awarded, although others certainly achieved similarly impressive hauls. According to his VC citation, Sgt Joseph Lister of the 1st Battalion, Royal Fusiliers, captured 'about a hundred of the enemy' during an attack 'east of Ypres' on 9 October 1917, albeit in slightly different circumstances to those experienced by Todger.[4]

Sgt Alvin York, the world-renowned American soldier and recipient of the Medal of Honour (America's equivalent to the VC), is credited with capturing 132 prisoners during the First World War. York, however, had the support of seventeen other men who assisted him by suppressing the enemy, which allowed him to advance and capture them. A number of these men were also decorated for their part in the round-up, confirming it as a team effort.

Many years later, in 1941, during the Second World War, a movie about Sgt York was released, thus propelling the American hero into the limelight and ultimate stardom. In England, upon the release of the movie, comparisons between York and Todger, both of whom had received their respective country's highest military honour for the capture of a large quantity of prisoners, were soon made.[5]

Before going any further, it is perhaps best to address the 'elephant in the room' and explain the origins of Pte Thomas Jones's somewhat peculiar and humorous nickname. The name of 'Todger' was spawned on the streets of Runcorn and was the result of the childish creativity of his friends when he was just a lad.

Tom, as he was commonly known, was a talented footballer and had a reputation as being very artful when getting past his opponents with the ball. His skilful style of play had earned him the nickname of 'Dodger', and it did not take long for his mates to seize on the opportunity. Dodger's newly-established nickname soon evolved. The initial of his Christian name ('T') was promptly combined with his nickname of 'Dodger', and the new nickname of 'Todger' was firmly established. The name stuck, and he was soon known as nothing else among his friends, although, perhaps not surprisingly, his parents did not buy into it and continued to call him Tom. Many years later, the name would follow him to France, and in an interview with a reporter following the awarding of his VC, Todger related that those at the front knew him by no other name.

Todger was a working-class man from the small industrial town of Runcorn that sits on the banks of the River Mersey in Cheshire. Prior to the war, as a young territorial, Todger had won acclaim for his accuracy on the shooting ranges and was considered the best shot of his detachment.

Like many of the townsfolk, he was swept up into the war. He proved to be a very capable soldier and his varied attributes and skillsets saw him utilised in a number of ways when he reached the front. He would be employed as a marksman and occasional sniper, as well as a guide and bomber. It also became quickly evident that he could handle himself more than adequately when involved in the close-quarter and often hand-to-hand fighting that trench warfare would bring. Time and time again, he would get to grips with the enemy, and each time, he would come out as the victor.

When Todger arrived on the Western Front in January 1915, he was able to quickly adapt to the harsh realities of war. Now in his mid-thirties, he went to great lengths to look after the younger soldiers in his platoon. His sense of humour and ability to remain cheerful under heavy barrages and other times of high stress cemented him as a very popular and irreplaceable member of the battalion, and his presence alone helped to inspire others to endure the many hardships that they continually suffered.

On one occasion, after having his rifle disabled during a heavy enemy bombardment, Todger calmly brewed up some tea and proceeded to move around the position under a torrent of shells, cheerily dishing it out to his frightened comrades. Acts such as this had a steadying effect on others and could not help but raise morale.

Highland Light Infantry Officer Capt. Douglas Cuddeford said that each platoon often had at least one 'bright and irresponsible' individual, 'whose good humour and lively wit provided the leaven that kept the majority cheerful under the most trying conditions'.[6]

Cuddeford's description sums up Todger to a tee. He was a well-known humorist who had the canny ability to maintain his 'lively wit' when under fire. Following the announcement of his VC, when the public were eager to hear about the man who had captured over 100 Germans, it was duly reported that his 'popularity among his comrades was at this time based on his fame as a humorist in camp and billet, [and] was inspired by the occasion to perpetrate a joke'.[7]

Like many heroes of the day, Todger, on occasion, would prove to be 'irresponsible' or slightly mischievous, and he later admitted: 'I did things I shouldn't have done, really'.[8]

For the most part, his lapses of soldierly conduct would take place when out of the line. A notable exception took place on 25 September 1916, when he disobeyed a direct order from his officer who had asserted that he was not to leave his position but was to consolidate where he was. Todger ignored the order, but since his refusal to obey it resulted in him receiving the VC, Todger can perhaps be forgiven for this display of indiscipline.

Todger would remain a private soldier for the duration of the war, but his leadership qualities extended far beyond what would be expected from a man holding that humble rank. His age, maturity, and experience as a pre-war territorial contributed towards moulding him into the soldier he was. But there was more to him than that, and his character and reckless courage played a far more important part in things to come. A lack of stripes did not in any way hinder Todger's willingness to lead men, nor did it affect his bravery or the personal risks he was willing to take.

The VC was not the only gallantry award that Todger received. Two years after his VC, for actions in September 1918, he would receive the Distinguished Conduct Medal (DCM) in an act that displayed his leadership skills, as well as a large dose of bravery.

Todger's VC was the first of just two to be awarded to the Cheshire Regiment; the other being to Hugh Colvin, who, as a second-lieutenant in the 9th Battalion, cleared several dugouts and captured fourteen prisoners and some machine guns 'East of Ypres' in September 1917.

With both the VC and DCM to his name, Todger is the most decorated member in the Cheshire Regiment, and since the regiment's amalgamation into the Mercian Regiment, this honour can never be surpassed.

Todger's VC thrust him into the spotlight where, to some extent, he would remain for the rest of his days. After his return from the war in 1919, he slipped back into civilian life with apparent ease, returning to his occupation as a fitter with no visible signs or lasting effects of the horrors that he had experienced and endured. He was instantly recognised by everyone in his hometown, and residents from all age groups were aware of his deeds.

Those who knew Todger remember a modest and unassuming man who, by all accounts, was content in taking a backseat in everyday life. This laid-back attitude was in stark contrast to the Todger Jones of the First World War where, as the bullets began to fly, he did the direct opposite of taking a back seat by volunteering for any dangerous task or enterprise.

Todger's feet remained firmly grounded, and he lived a quiet life, but the warrior spirit never left him. On the outbreak of the Second World War, this spirit once again revealed itself when Todger, who at the time was well into his sixties, attempted to enlist into the infantry, but, much to his disappointment, he was refused on account of his age.

Thomas Alfred Jones VC, DCM, died in 1956, but his name and deeds lives on.

1

Pre-War

In 1910, Runcorn was home to approximately 16,500 residents. Owing to an influx of people seeking steady, better paid, and guaranteed work within the town's industrial and manufacturing industry, this modest number was an increase on previous years. The town's industry was its biggest pull, and it was the prospect of favourable employment that had first tempted the Joneses to make it their home.

Soap manufacturing had begun in Runcorn in 1803 after the farmer, John Johnson, built a soap works in the town. Situated on the south side of the Bridge Water Canal, the business flourished for many years and was later taken over by his two sons, Thomas and John.

The ambitious brothers rapidly expanded the family empire and oversaw the construction of a chemical works based in Runcorn, a coal mine in St Helens, a salt works in Winsford, and some limestone quarries in North Wales. Subsequently, during the American Civil War (1861–65), their business empire would come crashing down. Huge profits had initially been made by supplying the Confederates, but an attempt to run the Union blockade caused heavy loss among their vessels, and the Battle of Charlestown ultimately finished them off.

Back in 1816, the Hazlehurst soap factory had also been established in the town, and following the decline of the Johnsons', they were able to expand into the manufacture of mottled soap, which was exported worldwide. During the later part of the nineteenth century, the town would become more and more dominated by chemical and tanning industries. These industries, together with the dockyards and sandstone extraction from the quarries, would prove to be the town's backbone.

Edward Jones, Todger's paternal grandfather (born *c.* 1811), made the move to Runcorn in the 1830s from Flintshire in North Wales where he had been a lead miner in the village of Halkyn. He quickly found employment in soap manufacturing and met Fanny Dunbabin (*c*. 1815–72). The couple married in 1837 and together they had six children, including Todger's father, who was also called Edward, born in 1843.[1]

After finishing his education, Todger's father gained employment at Hazlehurst's soap works where he would remain for his entire working life, completing an impressive sixty-two years with the company with hardly a day off sick. Edward was also a popular and long-standing member of the Oddfellow & Friendly Society, and he spent twenty years as a preacher at the local Ellesmere Street Free Church.

Edward Jones married Elizabeth Lawson at the Parish Church (St Lawrence) in the neighbouring town of Frodsham on 18 April 1868. They lived at 24 Princess Street in the heart of Runcorn in a modest two-bedroom terrace and later moved to No. 39. The claustrophobic confines of this 'two-up, two-down' must have been a squeeze. In total, Edward and Elizabeth would have nine children, although one, Lilly, would die in infancy in 1879.[2]

Todger was born in the family home in Princess Street on Christmas Day, 25 December 1880. He attended the old Runcorn National School (1885–94), which later became the Runcorn All Saints Parish Church School, located on Church Street—a mere stone's throw from his home.[3]

Todger possessed a natural aptitude for sports, which was something he enjoyed and thrived at as a child. He was particularly keen on football and was recognised as a talented player. The children of Runcorn had a good sense of humour. Todger's ability to skip around players when running with the ball earned him the nickname of 'Dodger', which, when combined with the initial of his Christian name, soon became 'Todger'. His young friends had inadvertently created a name that would stick with him for the rest of his life and beyond.

After leaving school in 1894, Todger gained employment as an apprentice fitter at Hazlehurst soap works working alongside his father. Following the completion of his apprenticeship, he went to work as a time-served fitter at the Salt Union Works in Western Point in Runcorn.

Todger had an active social life and was a member of the Liberal Club that was situated just a couple of streets from where he lived. He won a number of prizes playing billiards at the club. He was also keen on darts, and his love of football would later see him appointed honorary secretary for the Runcorn Reserves Football Club.

In January 1900, shortly after his twentieth birthday, Todger joined the Runcorn Volunteers—a local infantry unit that belonged to the 2nd (Earl of Chester's) Volunteer Battalion. The Second Boer War had begun the previous October, and a number of the Runcorn volunteers sailed to South Africa for active service.

Todger settled into the detachment very quickly and impressed his fellow volunteers with his displays of accuracy on the shooting range situated in the nearby Runcorn Hills by invariably beating everyone before him. He was soon considered to be the best shot in the unit, and he won a number of prizes for his first-class marksmanship.

Upon the formation of the Territorial Force in April 1908, the Runcorn Volunteers became a part of the Cheshire Regiment's 5th (Earl of Chester's) Battalion. Todger received the Territorial Force Efficiency Medal in 1912 upon the completion of twelve years' service.[4] He left the territorials the following year and, as regulations dictated, was placed on the National Reserve for a set period from where he could be called up again in the event of a national emergency. By 1913, the reserve body of the armed forces amounted to some 215,000 men. These men, come August 1914, would be recalled to the colours. Among their number would be the best shot in Runcorn.

2

The World Goes to War

The spark that ignited the First World War occurred when the heir to the Austrian Empire, Archduke Franz Ferdinand, was assassinated by Serbian nationalist Gavrilo Princip. Ferdinand and his wife, who was accompanying him, were shot down on the streets of Sarajevo on 28 June 1914 while travelling in an open-top car. Princip had no connections with the Serbian Government, but Austria-Hungary blamed them anyway and responded by issuing an ultimatum, which was promptly followed by preparations for war.

Tensions in Europe had been strained for a number of years, and events soon escalated and spiralled out of control. On 28 July, Austria declared war on Serbia. In response, Russia ordered the mobilisation of her army in support of Serbia, while Germany backed Austria. On 1 August, Germany declared war against Russia, and France mobilised in support of Russia.

Germany occupied Luxembourg, and in order to face the French, sought passage through independent Belgium, which, on 31 July, had mobilised its own army in anticipation of the looming crisis. Belgium called attention to the fact that Britain was honour-bound by treaty to defend Belgian neutrality, although Germany confidently hoped that Britain would not go to war 'over a scrap of paper'.[1]

Meanwhile, Belgium bluntly refused Germany's demands for passage, making it clear that they would defend their neutrality no matter what. Nevertheless, on 4 August, the German Army crossed the Belgian border to attack Liege. Britain immediately declared war on Germany, and its regiments, both in Britain and those stationed around the globe, hurriedly made preparations to go to war.

The Cheshire Regiment had been formed by the duke of Norfolk in Chester in 1689, although, at the time, they were known as the 22nd Regiment of Foot. Their symbol was the oak leaf, which was said to have originated as a result of the regiment's actions during the War of the Austrian Succession.

The story goes that a detachment of the regiment was present at the Battle of Dettingen on 27 June 1743. At one stage, King George II, who was on horseback leading his men into battle, galloped along the line of soldiers brandishing his sword. His horse, petrified by the noise of battle and the French cavalry that was charging towards them, panicked and bolted towards the enemy. Finding himself some distance ahead of the main body of British troops, the king found himself in imminent danger of falling into enemy hands or worse.

The Cheshire men were quick to react. As one, they rushed forward to protect their king. One soldier was able to grab the reins of the king's horse and bring it under control, while others formed around him. The French cavalry were successfully driven off, and the king, who was positioned under a great oak tree, then plucked one of its leaves and presented it to the officer commanding the 22nd Foot, telling him that they should wear it with pride as a mark of their gallantry.[2]

Dettingen was the last battle in which a British monarch personally led his troops into action.

Throughout their years of service, the regiment fought in numerous campaigns. They played a major roll in the Battle of Meeanee on 17 February 1843 where Sir Charles Napier's British East India Company defeated the Talpur Amir's of Sindh in what is now modern-day Pakistan.[3]

Due to their participation at Meeanee, their 'Regiment Day' is 17 February, and it is recognised and remembered each year with much pride within the regiment. A second regiment day was subsequently added after the battalion's actions at Mons on 24 August 1914, of which we will later hear more.

Since 1905, the Cheshire Regiment's 1st Battalion had been a part of the 5th Division's newly established 15th Infantry Brigade that had been formed at Fermoy in Ireland. At the time of its inception, the brigade, in addition to the Cheshires, consisted of the 1st Norfolks, 1st Bedfordshires, 1st Dorsets, and the 2nd Battalion Highland Light Infantry, although the structure would see various changes in the coming years.[4]

The 1st Cheshires had been stationed in Londonderry in Ireland for around two years before the outbreak of the First World War. Mobilisation had been swift, and by 10 August, they were fully mobilised and extremely excited at the prospect of going to war. The battalion entrained at Londonderry on the morning of 14 August and travelled to Belfast in two trains, one under the charge of CO Lt-Col. Boger and the other under 2iC Maj. Chetwynd-Stapyton. From Belfast, they boarded SS *Massilia* under sealed orders, unaware of their destination.

Once at sea, the orders were opened and a loud cheer erupted as their destination was revealed as France. Every man was given a printed message from Lord Kitchener with instructions to carry it in their personal pay books:

> You are ordered abroad as a soldier of the King to help our French comrades against the invasion of a common enemy. You have to perform a task which will need your courage, your energy, your patience. Remember that the honour of the British Army depends on your individual conduct. It will be your duty not only to set an example of discipline and perfect steadiness under fire, but also to maintain the most friendly relations with those whom you are helping in this struggle. The operations in which you are engaged will, for the most part, take place in a friendly country, and you can do your own country no better service than in showing yourself in France and Belgium in the true character of a British soldier.[5]

The message also instructed the soldiers to 'be invariably courteous, polite and kind', while not doing anything that risked injury to civilians or destruction to property.[6] Kitchener also warned them to refrain from a variety of temptations, such as looting, wine, and women.

Lastly, the battalion were instructed 'to set an example of discipline and perfect steadiness under fire'.[7] Just days after their arrival in France, the battalion would have the opportunity to fulfil this obligation, and they would carry it out to the letter.

The battalion landed at Le Havre with the British Expeditionary Force (BEF) on 16 August 1914. Accompanying them was their beloved miniature colour. As with all colours, it was considered a most sacred and cherished possession, epitomising the regiment it represented.

The miniature colour was a relatively new creation. It had been stitched in 1911 by the wives of the officers at the request of then-CO Lt-Col. Kellie, who had asked if they could create a perfect miniature version of their colour. The wives had eagerly obliged and the result was an exact replica of their full-sized colour, measuring one-quarter of its size. The miniature colour was presented to the company who had won the annual shooting competition. Every year, each of the four companies competed for the honour of having in their care. The winning company would then fiercely defend the right to retain it in the next tournament, while the other three companies attempted to win it for themselves. In 1914, 'B' Company had won the competition. As such, it was they who proudly carried it with them to war.

The story of the Cheshire Regiment's miniature colour, together with the battalion's actions on 24 August 1914, is a source of great pride within the regiment.

After disembarking at Le Havre, the battalion had marched countless miles. By 24 August, they were in Audregnies in Belgium, dog-tired after a forced march. They had been rushed into place at the last minute and, as a consequence, had no idea of their surroundings or the lay of the land. Nevertheless, the battalion was ordered to act as a rear-guard and to hold their ground while their division retired in conjunction with a general retirement.

Faced with overwhelming odds, the Cheshires doggedly stuck to their position. Eventually, orders were sent for them to extract and fall back, but the message never got through. Several other messages were sent, but none of them arrived. Presumably, the runners tasked with the job had become casualties or were unable to reach them.

By the end of the day, the battalion had virtually ceased to exist. They had gone into action with twenty-seven officers and 933 men. By the end of the day, just six officers, a warrant officer, and 199 men, including the transport section that had been kept out of the battle, remained to answer the roll call.[8]

Drummer Baker of 'B' Company was the man entrusted with the miniature colour, and he was under no illusions as to the importance of his task. With the German infantry on all sides, and their resistance disintegrating, Baker had realised he would in all probability be killed or captured, and whatever the outcome, the colour would then fall to the enemy. Baker was not particularly keen on this prospect.

Amid the battle, Baker ran to a nearby house (sometimes referred to as a 'barn'), burst through the door, scaled the stairs to the attic, and hid the colour under the eaves behind some straw. By hand signals, he begged the startled inhabitants to keep the colour hidden while trying his utmost to enforce the importance of his request upon them. He tried to make it clear that they were not to hand it over to anyone other than an Englishman.

With the colour tucked away, Baker left the house and returned to the fight. He was captured shortly after, but not before he had confided in a comrade, Pte Riley, about what he had done with the colour. Despite being wounded, Riley managed to evade capture and make a successful break out from the encircling Germans. Riley's survival and escape meant that the remnants of the battalion had knowledge of Baker's efforts in saving the colour, although the facts were far from clear.

The territory was taken by the Germans and would remain in their hands for the duration the war. Now, the Cheshire's could only hope that their colour would not be discovered.

As a reservist, Todger was one of the first men to present himself at the Runcorn Drill Hall on the morning of 5 August, the day after Britain had declared war on Germany.[9]

Due to his occupation, Todger wanted to join the Royal Engineers, but as a reservist, he was earmarked to remain in the infantry. He attested in Birkenhead on 31 August and was given the regiment number of 11000, as a private in the 1st Battalion, Cheshire Regiment. His papers record him weighing 126 lb and standing at 5 feet 6 inches, with a 'good' physical development. He was thirty-four years old.

On the day of Todger's attestation, a large draft that had been sent overseas from the regimental depot in Chester, arrived in France to bolster the depleted numbers of their 1st Battalion who were licking their wounds after their last stand at Audregnies. George Dunning, who lived near to Todger in Runcorn and worked locally as a labourer, was one of those to arrive.[10]

Like many of the replacements who joined their comrades in the field, Dunning was soon killed. He was among the heavy losses sustained by the battalion at La Bassée in October and, together with reservist Joseph Jones, who had been killed on 24 August, was one of the first men from Runcorn to be killed in the war.

On the 22nd alone, the battalion lost eight officers and 220 other ranks, which all but neutralised their draft of three officers and 250 other ranks that had arrived to boost their numbers just days earlier. The men, it seemed, were dropping just as fast as they were arriving. The sense of loss was not restricted to the other ranks, and many officers were also killed. A sense of their casualties can be gleaned from *Ever Glorious*, an important regimental publication, which solemnly recorded: 'It is a sad and sufficient commentary to note that in this month of Oct. the Battalion had no less than seven commanding officers'.[11]

The battalion came out of the trenches at Ypres on 21 November with just three officers and 230 other ranks. They were in a poor state of health and rheumatism was rife. Almost every man suffered from swollen feet and knees and many of the men were described as 'quite crippled'.[12] As the year came to an end, the soldiers who had sailed with the original BEF in August were few and far between.

Meanwhile, Todger and those other reservists who had yet to sail for the front were employed with the Mersey Defence Force, guarding vital areas that were considered vulnerable to German infiltration. While batches of men continued to depart for overseas service, further training continued to take place at Codford in Wiltshire.

In January 1915, Todger found himself one of almost 250 men sent as reinforcements to France. They landed at Le Havre on 16 January 1915 before travelling to Bailleul. Several days later, they linked up with the battalion who were out of the line in Divisional Reserve. A further 109 reinforcements arrived the following week before the battalion were ordered into the line at the relatively quite sector of Wulverghem, giving the recently-arrived members of the battalion a gentle introduction to war and the time to acclimatise themselves to life in the trenches.

It was not until March—when the battalion took over some of the trenches at St Eloi—that Todger and his fellow replacements experienced war at it harshest. Until this point, only a trickle of casualties had been sustained by shellfire during their various stints in the trenches. Mostly they had been out of the line and in reserve while they were brought up to somewhere near full strength.

The Cheshires held International Trench on the east side of the Ypres–Comines Canal between 'The Mound' and 'The Bluff' where a curious situation existed. The British and Germans were both holding the same trench, and a number of scantily built 'blocks' were the only thing separating the opposing soldiers. Fighting here was very lively, particularly since the Germans had a habit of sweeping the British section with machine-gun fire throughout both day and night. This fire caused a high number of casualties, particularly when reliefs were taking place. Enemy artillery also wreaked havoc, and the British sections were knocked about a great deal. In typical Tommy humour, 'some wag suggested that the repairs should be undertaken by each side on alternate days!'[13]

On 14 March, following a bombardment and the explosion of a mine under 'The Mound', German infantry attacked and captured St Eloi. A counterattack during the night succeeded in re-establishing all of the lost ground, excluding 'The Mound', which the Germans were able to retain. No further attempts were made to push the British out, and 'after a short period of liveliness, conditions returned to normal'.[14]

'Normal' meant the usual stagnation of trench warfare and, as a matter of course, the inevitable daily wastage that came with it. On 28 March, Capt. Thomas Frost became one such casualty after being shot in the head by a sniper. He was the son of Alderman John Frost, the mayor of Chester, and he had recently been given command of a company. As a member of the original BEF, he had been at war since the start, and was one of the only officers in the battalion to get through 1914.

Todger had been speaking with Frost just before he was shot and was one of the last men to see him alive.

At this point, the battalion considered their time in the trenches to be relatively quiet. Nevertheless, there had been several incidents of note for Todger, whose ability to transition from peacetime reserve to an actively serving soldier was deemed very swift. He had been appointed as a guide almost as soon as he had arrived with the battalion, and he handled this responsible roll admirably, earning a good reputation among his comrades for his ability to lead them through mazes of trenches in the dark. Todger wrote very detailed accounts of his first couple of months on the Western Front, describing shellfire and enemy sniper fire, among other things.

In a letter to a friend that was subsequently forwarded for publication in the *Runcorn Guardian*, on 9 April 1915, Todger wrote:

> I have often thought of the promise to write you, but this is about the first chance I have had. Well, I suppose you want to know how things are as we see them over here. The first trenches I went in were only thirty five yards from the Huns, so you may realise for yourself how alert we had to be. You dare not show your head above the top in the day time. If you did you soon got one in the 'cannister'. We caught the Huns just coming over to attack once, but they did not get five yards.

> Next day we, in our company, perceived a party working in the rear of their trenches and we soon had them over. They saw the company from which the fire came and shelled it all day. The fire was so severe that they knocked the sandbags off the top and fairly rolled them over. At night we put up about 50 new ones, but we had to put more up next day. The N.C.O. in charge helped me to get them up and when he was 'batting' them down with a spade the Huns took pot shots at it. They hit it about three times. The N.C.O. went to the next company and got his head over the top to fire. He fired four rounds, but they had him 'set' and got him through the centre of the head.
>
> The next night the rifle fire was the heaviest there has been on that front. Bullets were flying about like hailstones from the front and right and left. Everybody was glad when day dawned so we could rest a little. There is practically no firing in the daytime unless somebody shows himself. After we had done our eight days we went for a rest for eight. Afterwards we returned to the same front, which, by the way, is the most advanced portion in the whole 330 miles. We had only to hold it, as we were waiting for the flanks to be broken before we advanced. Instead of doing our eight we had to do 18, and I can tell you it was a very rough time–rain, snow and frost, but at last a relief brigade came up. To the delight of the Runcorn lads we found the 5th Cheshires were in it. At night we went to see the Runcorn Company, and you may guess we had a pleasant time with them.[15]

On 16 March, after a 'quiet day in the trenches', the battalion had been relieved and moved to Vlamertinge before marching to Ypres, where they had arrived on the evening of the 21st:

Todger continued:

> Next we were marched about six miles to our billets, and, after four days there, we received orders to get on the move again. We marched about 16 miles to another front, where the fighting had been, and still is, very severe. The roads here are horrible to get along; badly made and over show tops in slush—sometimes up to your knees. We rested for the night in some huts. Next day we went another six miles and took our position in the trenches, where we are doing 'two in and two out' at present. We have lost a good many men here. It is very bad ground for us and very dirty.[16]

In the letter to his friend, Todger went on to describe going out to look for a missing NCO. His love of souvenirs is also very evident:

> The last time up I have been guiding to a certain trench which we occupy at dusk and come out at dawn. It is a very trying job and also very risky. You can realize what it is. A strange country and you have only been in the

> trenches once when you are told off to guide your different companies each night, as black as the ace of spades, and woods to pass through. The least slip and you get them cut up. The bullets whistle past you something awful and seem to come from all directions. The other guide with me got wounded so it made it worse for me with the parties I took in. We were very lucky and only lost one.
>
> One night an N.C.O. went on his own with a message when I was away. When I got back the officer was uneasy about him and asked me to go to see if I could find him in a certain place. I went there and found that he had left 45 minutes before, so I went to look for him off the roads. I wandered about for a while [for about 2,000 yards], but could not see him. Then I stepped through a gap in a hedge and got a bit of a shock. A starlight went up and there on the ground I saw three Germans. I whipped up my rifle and was just going to have a clout for it when I noticed that they had not moved. When the next light went up I saw their packs and coats were covered with frost and I knew then that they were dead. I then thought of souvenirs and was just going to take their helmets and rifles when another light went up. I was quickly flat on my back and wriggling into a ditch. I had got between our lines and theirs.
>
> They had 'spotted' me, and the bullets flew all round me, knocking up the earth.... I was in a fix, and lay in the ditch, wondering how I was going to get out of it. They fired for about five minutes, and sent light after light up. They must have thought they had got me, for they stopped for a minute. It was my chance, and I did 'even time' across the field back again. I found a hedge and crawled along that, and eventually got to a path I knew. I went to the station and, just as I was going back to the trench to report it, in walked the missing N.C.O. It turned out he had been down with a message to the C.O. and did not leave word where he was going. I was travelling about all that night, and I don't want another like it for a long time. I am just going to relieve now. I am on guard and the candle is about 'fed up'.[17]

Todger's natural instinct as a guide was soon recognised by his comrades, including Pte Newton who, on one occasion, wrote: 'Tom Jones was our guide from the trenches the other night when our Relieving Party got it hot, and he deserves all praise for it, as it is all done in the dark, over fields and through woods, and we didn't lose a man'.[18]

Todger ended his own letter with the following words:

> Thanks for the kindness in sending the eggs. They have gone astray somewhere, but I appreciate it, and wish they would turn up. J. Royle has been taken very ill, and Dutton, of Western Point has a slight wound in the head, but is otherwise all right, and can walk about. I hope you and all the boys are in the pink.[19]

Incidentally, a letter from Royle featured directly under Todger's letter in the newspaper. Royle describes his experiences since landing in France, the snowstorms that they had endured and the enemy snipers that he, along with the weather, considered the worst threat. He made no mention of being 'very ill', as was mentioned by Todger in his own letter.

As new arrivals at Ypres, the Cheshires had yet to fully experience the horrors it evoked, but at Hill 60, they were soon to find out.

3

Hill 60: 'One of my Hottest Trials'

Situated a few miles south-east of Ypres, Hill 60 was one of three man-made features created from excavated spoils from the construction of the Ypres–Comines railway in the 1850s. It was 230 metres wide and 46 metres high, and it sat on the highest point of a gradual 1,800-metre rise. It was a crucial and domineering position, and whoever held it had a truly advantageous and commanding view over the Ypres Salient.

The two other features created from the railway spoils were smaller in size. These were 'The Caterpillar', named as such due to its shape, and 'The Dump', which was the smallest of the three features. They sat to the south and to the west of Hill 60, respectively.

The importance of Hill 60 was not lost to either side. For this reason, it was the scene of heavy fighting throughout the war. The Germans had captured it during First Battle of Ypres in November 1914, retaining possession until 17 April 1915 when six British mines, planted by tunnellers of the Royal Engineers were detonated—two directly under the hill and a further three in its immediate area. The hill was then taken with comparatively little loss to the British attackers, although the force of the explosions caused some friendly casualties in the 5th Division.

Severe fighting took place over the next few days as each side tried to extend and solidify their lines. Mazes of trenches were bitterly contested, and thousands of shell holes were fought over, with savage fighting taking place in the mine craters as both sides tussled for their possession. The Germans attacked with massed infantry and also carried out a series of smaller bombing attacks, but their efforts were repulsed.

The Second Battle of Ypres began on 22 April 1915. That day, at 5.30 p.m., the Germans, using 5,500 cylinders, released some 168 tonnes of chlorine gas towards the unsuspecting British and their allies. Primarily, it was directed towards French Senegalese colonial troops to the left of the British trenches. The sight of this thick yellowish-green gas cloud drifting towards them was perplexing. This was the first time that chlorine gas had been used as a weapon of war, and no preventative measures were in place.[1]

The gas caused confusion and a mass panic, resulting in the abandonment of the trenches and a large 4-mile gap in the line, but the Germans—themselves weary of the gas—failed to exploit the advantage it had given them. Potential disaster was averted when the Canadian 1st Division, together with units of French troops, rushed in to plug the gap.

The gas attack was met with widespread disgust and caused an outrage in Britain. Nonetheless, Britain quickly began carrying out experiments to use their own gas as retaliation and to keep on par with the forever advancing weapons of war. As chance would have it, the first gas used by British forces in September 1915 during the Battle of Loos would be manufactured in the chemical yards of Runcorn.

Within days of the gas release, British soldiers received instructions on how to lessen the effects should they find themselves in its midst. The advice was to urinate on to (or 'wet') a cloth and to breathe through it. This was far from ideal, but until a more suitable and permanent solution could be found, it would have to do.

The Cheshires were lucky to escape the next gas attack that took place on the evening of 1 May. Their division was holding the hill, but it was the 1st Dorsets who bore the brunt of it on their brigade's sector. When it was launched, the Cheshires received news that the 'situation on N.E. front of YPRES salient [was] critical and provisional orders for withdrawal were issued'.[2]

Before they had moved into the line, the 1st Dorsets had been provided with makeshift respirators. In essence, these were nothing more than flannels and gauzes with instructions to wet them before use if a gas cloud came over. The Dorsets's sentries had little time to raise the alarm before being enveloped in the deadly fumes. The gas took immediate effect with disastrous results. 'It is difficult for any man to keep his head under such circumstances,' wrote the author of the Dorsetshire Regiment history, 'and the men crouched down at the bottom of the trench only to be completely asphyxiated'.[3]

Soon, very few men in the forward line were in any fit state to offer any resistance. The Dorsets's reserves rushed forward to assist as the German infantry attacked up old communication trenches in an attempt to bomb them off the hill. Many men suffered harrowing deaths. Maj. Cowie arrived to find the 'deep and narrow trenches blocked with dead, with many others dying in terrible agony.'[4] Another officer of the Dorsets was 'absolutely sickened by it', writing in a letter home: 'Clean killing is at least comprehensive, but this murder by slow agony absolutely knocks me'.[5]

In relation to the initial capture of Hill 60 and the subsequent bouts of fighting, Lt Arthur Greg, a young bombing officer in the Cheshires, explained the battalion's experience:

> Eighteen days in a fire trench with heavy engagements only a few hundred yards to our right, and more critical fighting a mile or so on our left, was not calculated to act as nerve tonic. Our trenches had rocked and swayed under the shock of six successive explosions that had blown up so many of His Imperial Majesty's Bavarian troops, and had altered the features of what had once been known as Hill 60. We had been listening for days to the unending shriek of missiles that were angrily hurled over our heads on the unfortunate town of Ypres.[6]

It had been recognised and acknowledged that the battalion had been either at or near the front for an overly long period of time, and on numerous occasions they had been promised a rest, but subsequent events, chiefly the German gas and infantry attacks, had scuppered these plans. Instead, they had been ordered to remain close at hand in order to be rushed into the line if needed. Finally, on 4 May, the Cheshires moved into reserve. 'At last', exclaimed a jovial Arthur Greg, 'we were going back to rest!'[7]

The battalion moved to dug-outs to the south-west of Zillebeke Lake where they arrived on the evening of the 4th thoroughly worn out. But their time in reserve would prove to be short-lived.

On the morning of 5 May, the Germans launched another gas attack against Hill 60. Once again, it was the unfortunate Dorsets who stood in its path, and the Cheshires received word that they were urgently required to assist.

In describing their move forward, Arthur Greg wrote:

> As soon as we were well in the open we extended and proceeded, expecting any moment to be fired on by some concealed Germans. We passed almost under the very guns of one of our field batteries. They were pounding away at high pressure and seemed almost as excited as we were. It was rather a comfort to get past that spot as the Germans were answering their fire with considerable vigour.
>
> After a good many halts, we finally came to the end of that shell-swept two miles of open country. It was piping hot and we were terribly thirsty. The sights we saw on the way up were not calculated to cheer us much. We passed many groups of men dead or dying, some wounded, and all badly gassed. Most of them were writhing in awful agony. The colour of their faces and the noise they made turned out blood cold. We could do nothing for them. We had to push on, leaving them gasping for breath and dying under that pitiless sun.[8]

Todger later provided his own account of this journey under enemy fire:

> We had only been relieved the night before, and wanted a rest badly, but at ten o'clock in the morning we received word that something had happened at Hill 60, and it was up to us to try to set it right. We got through Ypres town to the

> railway cutting, and there came under heavy shell fire. Bad wasn't the word for it, for they were bowling the lads over right and left, and as we got closer and closer their machine-gun fire was mowing us down something cruel.[9]

The railway cutting offered Todger and his comrades some degree of shelter. They donned their 'gas masks' under the cover it provided.

German infantry had followed up behind the gas towards the British lines and had made excellent progress, infiltrating the front-line trenches at various points around the hill. At the cutting, the Cheshires encountered large numbers of enemy infantry advancing four deep up the railway line. With a yell, the Cheshires immediately charged. In the face of this determined attack, the Germans that were not killed turned tail and ran.

The situation as it stood was far from clear, but the appearance of German infantry on the railway confirmed that at least some part of the British forward trenches had been overrun.

A defensive flank from the front line to the Eastern edge of Larch Wood was formed. Lt-Col. Scott then formed up two companies between the railway and the Zwartelen road before issuing the order to advance. But, as he did so, Scott slumped to the ground mortally wounded.

Lt-Col. Arthur De Courcey Scott was an officer with twenty years' service in the regiment. He had arrived from the 2nd Battalion on 22 February and had served with distinction through the Boer War. He had been stationed with his battalion in India on the outbreak of the First World War, but they had been quickly summoned back to England. They had arrived home on Christmas Eve 1914 before sailing for France the following month. Scott's arrival had been met with widespread delight by the men of the 1st Battalion, who recognised they had a man whose heart beat only for the regiment.

Scott was hugely popular with the men, and they were filled with rage when they saw him fall. Todger confirmed this in one of his own accounts and explained that they did not wait for any further orders, but 'saw red' and reacted instinctively.[10]

Their blood was up. With a wild yell, and without instruction, they charged at the Germans and succeeded in fighting their way through the first line of resistance. With momentum at a high, they continued the attack, taking a second and then a third line.

With the enemy ejected, they took stock of the situation. A quick look at the bodies, both British and German lying thick on the ground, testified to the desperation and ferocity of the fighting that had taken place.

They came upon a number of Dorset men in a trench. Todger noticed they seemed to be staring at him without expression. He and his comrades spoke up: '"Matey, you've been relieved", we said to one, but there was no answer. "There's some hot tea waiting for you in Ypres", we said to another. No answer'.[11]

It quickly dawned on them that something was drastically wrong. 'They were dead—gassed', said Todger, 'and we didn't know then of the diabolical device that had killed them'.[12]

It is difficult to believe that Todger and his comrades 'didn't know' of the gas attack when evidence shows they were clearly aware of what they were dealing with. It is possible that Todger was referring to the fact that they had yet to experience it for themselves, and as such 'didn't know' of it first-hand.

The battalion war diary for this period suffers from an extreme shortage of detail. There is no mention of the heavy fighting that took place, nor is there mention of casualties, but this is perhaps understandable given the stresses at the time and the lack of officers present. In summing up the action, the war diarist simply wrote that they 'drove some of the enemy from vicinity of LARCH WOOD' and its support trenches.[13] The diary goes on to briefly mention an attack carried out by the King's Own Scottish Borderers, who 'attacked Hill 60 but without success'.[14]

In fact, a party of bombers belonging to the Cheshires were also heavily engaged during the night, although the diary makes no mention of it. Todger was one of those bombers.

4

A Bombing Attack

Lt Arthur Greg was a twenty-year-old officer attached to the 1st Cheshires from the regiment's 3rd (Reserve) Battalion. Like Todger, he had arrived with the battalion in January 1915, following a brief secondment to the 2nd Sherwood Foresters. His father, Ernest William Greg, was a longstanding officer with twenty-five years' service behind him who had commanded the regiment's 7th Battalion.

Arthur Greg was a bombing officer, an appointment that placed him at the forefront of the action with his bombers, exchanging grenades with his German counterparts. After playing a leading role in the battalion's counterattack as they charged Hill 60, his next task was to clear the communication trenches and fire trenches of the mangled corpses. It was an exhausting and somewhat gruesome job, which he and his men carried out 'till they nearly dropped'.[1]

The situation was made all the worse by the fact that the location of the enemy was obscure, although it was evident that some were to their rear. 'Sometimes we were fired on at close range from somewhere behind,' wrote Greg. 'The Germans had broken through and were still breaking through. Nobody quite knew where the next English troops on our left were.'[2]

The left was completely 'up in the air'. At one point, while going about their task of removing the dead, Greg and his party observed a number of men about 70 yards away, steadily making their way towards them. With shells landing all around and smoke filling the air, their vision was obscured and it was assumed—wrongly as it turned out—that the approaching soldiers were survivors from another regiment that had been originally holding the position. The approaching men were quickly shot down when their identity was finally revealed as German.

The situation was very confused, and nobody knew whether or not the next parapet contained British or German soldiers. Artillery from both sides fired where they thought enemy soldiers were positioned, but according to Greg: 'We were shelled by our own guns. The Germans were shelled by theirs'.[3]

The sight of German shovels at work and sandbags being thrown on top of the trenches told the Cheshires that the Germans were consolidating their position. In response, several marksmen began to take shots at any German who happened to show himself. 'C' Company arrived while this was in progress and, after forcing their way through the crowded trench, headed off to secure the left flank. Greg was then ordered to take a party of bombers and push on ahead of the position on the left and into the unknown.

In a somewhat understated version of events, Todger, when later explaining what happened, said:

> I was one of forty-three who went out that night to bomb the Germans, expecting that another regiment would take over the trenches from which we had driven the enemy.
>
> We used up all our bombs, and the Germans began to bomb us in turn. Our lieutenant was the only man with a revolver, and he used it until he had no more ammunition left and was shot.[4]

The 'lieutenant' in Todger's account was Arthur Greg, who was the only officer present during the enterprise. Greg would indeed be shot, but not before he and his party had taken part in a brutal and prolonged bombing fight that lasted through the night and into the next morning.

Greg himself takes up the story:

> We started. Suddenly out of one of the communication trenches one of 'C' Company officers appeared alone. He seemed quite cheerful but very tired. He had been doing a little investigation of his own and informed me that if I kept along my present path I should be into the Germans in another 40 yards. We pushed on, however. I was in front....
>
> The trench had been badly shattered and was lined with the curious yellow colour that spells lyddite. The trench was full of fresh German dead piled over each other. A lucky shell of ours had done its work and slaughtered about 20 Germans. We crawled over these. They were very wobbly and the going was bad. On turning round a traverse a bullet hit the sand bag just beside my face. I looked up and saw a dirty unshaven German staring at me with a rifle in his hand. He was shooting over a barricade. The range was about 10 yards. I withdrew and took cover behind a corpse. There were many Mauser rifles lying about and plenty of ammunition. I loaded and peeped over the corpse. We both fired simultaneously and both bobbed down again. It was a weird sort of duel. Neither of us cared much about it. Then, from my prostrate position, I started making a little barricade of my own. My friend behind the barricade had several more shots and so had I, but although hideously close, they did not take effect. This duel must end. It wasn't good enough. I think we both realised this

> about the same time, as my adversary didn't expose himself any more when I was looking.[5]

Greg then pushed forward ahead of his men, but they soon arrived to back him up:

> I passed the word for sandbags to be filled and passed up. In this way I was able to build a sort of barricade. I then withdrew a few yards and piled up what bodies I could with the help of two of my men against the barricade. We had to keep very low as shots came from behind, from the flank and from the front. It was an unhealthy spot, and I didn't like the carpet of Bavarian bodies; their limbs were so horribly arranged and their shoulders didn't make a firm footing. After leaving some good men near the barricade, I managed to plunge along past men and corpses to the healthier end...[6]

Greg lit a smoke and discussed the situation with his sergeant. The party then strengthened their position by barricading as best they could in case of a counterattack.

Greg then made what he described as 'the biggest blunder of any'.[7] He hurled two bombs at the Germans. His actions prompted an angry response:

> There seemed to be some confusion behind those sandbags in front of me and my men were vastly pleased. It was not long, however, before we got a full dose of those horrid little black grenades that Germans fling so accurately. For the next half hour or so we had a great duel. Many of my men were unfortunately hit.[8]

Attracted by the noise of battle, an officer belonging to the Dorsets came rushing up to see if he could help. Greg, who was engaged in a furious exchange of bombs with the Germans, shouted to him for more bombs. The officer struggled to him with a full box, but his head was blown clean off just as he was handing them over to Greg, who could not help but feel a pang of guilt at having urgently demanded the grenades.

As darkness descended, the party had been reduced to less than half its original strength. Some had been killed, while others had been forced to retire through wounds or through feeling the effects of gas that had been inhaled earlier in the day. The remaining men were spread thinly at various junctions in the maze of trenches, acting as sentries in case the Germans attempted a flanking move or attacked from some other unknown route.

A British barrage opened up around 9 p.m., flying over their heads and landing in and around the positions held by the Germans, suggesting an attack was imminent. Confirming their suspicions, a captain belonging to the 2nd King's Own Scottish Borderers arrived at the head of two companies and informed

Greg's party that they would be 'going over' from their position at 10 p.m. They attacked at the allotted time and swung to the right, but it did not go well:

> They were met with a storm of rifle and machine gun fire from the hill. Our artillery had not yet stopped and soon theirs started. The poor Scots were simply blown back with lead. They started again and went half-left. Their wounded were pouring into my trenches. The sounds were terrible, men shrieking, the fierce crackle of machine gun fire, and the cruel shriek of shrapnel. This was battle.[9]

Both companies ('C' and 'D') of the KOSB suffered horrendous casualties. According to their regiment history, 'C' Company were 'crushed instantaneously by heavy fire,' while 'D,' although reaching their objective, came under enfilade fire from 'The Caterpillar' before being bombed out at close range.[10]

Greg's isolated party witnessed just the KOSB going into action, but their attack was part of a larger one involving three battalions:

> About 9 p.m. three Battalions of the 13th Brigade came up from Ouderdom with orders to counter-attack and re-take the Hill. These troops had only been withdrawn from the fighting North of Ypres on the 4th, the units had not been made up to strength, and the men were far from fresh. The counter-attack was arranged to take place at 10 p.m., after a twenty minute Artillery bombardment. The night was dark, and this, and the irregularities of the position, rendered the forming up extremely difficult. At 10 p.m. the attack was launched, the K.O.S.B. on the right directed on the Hill, and the K.O.Y.L.I. [King's Own Yorkshire Light Infantry] on the left directed on the position thence to Zwartelen. The bombardment had been ineffective, and the K.O.S.B. were soon held up by rifle and machine-gun fire. On the left the K.OY.L.I. formed up, and attacked from a position in rear of the Cheshires, with the result that some confusion occurred; after a short delay they continued their advance. What actually occurred is not quite clear; some were driven back, but the greater part of two Companies completely disappeared.[11]

Half an hour after the abortive attack, a body of men approached the bombing party from the rear. Greg and his men were relieved to see they were wearing British service caps and they relaxed in the knowledge that German infantry had not worked their way round behind them. Unfortunately, the approaching soldiers were not as quick in their identification. The officer leading the approaching men suddenly shouted out, 'now boys, in at em!'[12]

The new arrivals charged at the Cheshire men with their bayonets fixed and set to work, stabbing and thrusting at their misidentified comrades. The Cheshires cried out frantically, 'working miracles' to make themselves 'recognised as friends'.[13] There were casualties, but it could have been worse, and Greg for one was thankful 'there was not more damage done'.[14]

The congested trench was a scene of pandemonium and the sound of laughter emanating from the German position left the crowded occupants under no illusions that the enemy found their plight highly amusing.

The party remained at their post throughout the night and into the morning. They had not eaten for over twenty-four hours and were now suffering a great deal from hunger. A quick scavenge produced some stale bread and other edible bits and pieces, and they were able to satisfy their stomachs to some degree.

It was while endeavouring to clear some mangled corpses from the trench that Lt Greg was finally shot. The bullet, fired by an eagle-eyed sniper, smashed into his face without warning:

> I went down like a log and was next aware of a loose, horrid and disconnected feeling about the lower part of my face. I was bleeding like a fountain and my mouth seemed full of obstacles. I tried to spit them out and found they were my teeth....
>
> My servant then applied all the bandages and field dressing he could find. I watched his horrified face with interest and noticed that everybody that saw me looked strangely at me. I then stumbled down the trench. I heard the shout everywhere, 'Make way, it's an officer.' I was at the time in my shirt sleeves with no hat and covered in blood. Some of the Jocks recognised me and said 'It's that Cheshire officer that's got hit.' I heard everything, I noticed everything, especially the looks on peoples faces.[15]

Greg would survive, but his wound looked ghastly and he was losing a lot of blood—the bullet having passed straight through his face near his jaw. With the assistance of his servant, Greg stumbled to the rear. He would later reach a large dugout that was being used as a dressing station, and after initial treatment, he would be sent back to England.

Many months later, despite being permanently disfigured and after coming through a long and trying recovery process, Greg would return to the war. In November 1915, he was promoted to the rank of captain. He joined the Royal Flying Corps, and in 1917, returned to the Western Front with the 55th Squadron. On 23 April, Greg and his observer, Robert Robson, took part in a bombing raid on a target in Lechelle and on an ammunition factory in Étreux. On the return flight, their formation of eight DH.4 bombers, one of which was flown by Greg, and five Martinsyde Elephants, which were being escorted by four Nieuports, were attacked by a large formation of Albatros D.III Scouts. Greg's machine was badly shot about in the ensuing battle, and both he and Robson were severely wounded. Despite his wounds, Greg descended from 18,000 feet and managed a successful landing in Allied lines. He died later that day, aged twenty-one.

His observer, Robson, lingered for almost a month before succumbing to his wounds.[16] Notification of Greg's death appeared in the *Cheshire Observer* on 5 May 1917, at which point, it had been two years to the day since he had gone into action with Todger at Hill 60.[17]

Sadly, Col. Greg's devastation at the loss of his son would be further compounded when, on 3 May 1918, his second son, Robert, died of wounds after an enemy shell scored a direct hit on his dugout. In keeping with family tradition, the teenager had been serving as a second-lieutenant in the Cheshire Regiment.[18]

Todger always gave praise when he considered it due. Regarding Arthur Greg, he thought him a brave young officer. Following his swift departure from the battlefield, Greg was initially reported as 'missing'. The fighting at the time was very confused, and owing to them not being with the main body of the battalion, and the fact that Greg had rushed off to the dressing station without returning, it is perhaps understandable how Greg came to be listed as 'missing'.

It may even have been Todger himself who reported Greg's whereabouts as unknown. The party had been whittled down to a mere handful of men. Todger was still with them, miraculously unwounded. A lone NCO found himself in charge. He asked Todger to get them out. 'All except three of us and a corporal were either killed or wounded,' Todger reported, 'and the corporal asked me if I could lead them back':

> I did it, and reported to the company officer, who said he had received reports on which he was going to recommend me for honours. A brave officer—reported from that very day as missing, as was the lieutenant.[19]

That Todger, a mere private soldier, reported to the company commander—above, or the very least, alongside, his corporal—is just one of a number of examples that show his leadership qualities. The bombing attack was also one of a number of occasions where Todger was earmarked for a gallantry award, only for it not to materialise owing to the officer who was to recommend him becoming a casualty before writing it up. His comrades would testify that on several occasions his actions had warranted a decoration but either his deeds had not been witnessed by officers or the officer who was to recommend him was killed before he could do so.

The general concept was for a battalion to spend four days in the frontline trench, followed by another four in reserve and then four at rest. This was the 'ideal scenario', but owing to circumstance, it was not always feasible and men often found themselves in or near to the front line for much longer periods, although this was counterbalanced by long periods out of it.

The Cheshires spent a monumental period 'in the trenches' during their time at Hill 60, which, according to Todger (commenting in 1916), 'constitutes a record either in the French or British Army for continual fire-trench work':

> We were at Hill 60 when it was blown up, and we remained in the trenches for twenty days, and after just one night out put in another forty-three days.... We were even reduced to the necessity of sewing sandbags together to serve as a change of 'linen'.[20]

On 30 June, the battalion was informed that it would be relieved during the next night. The promise of relief had been made more than once before. As such, 'this news was received with general incredulity by the men, who have to-day completed their 41st consecutive day in the trenches, and have come to look upon them as their normal residence'.[21]

When later recounting his time in the war, Todger would describe Hill 60 as one of his 'hottest trials'. It had been a stark contrast to what he and his comrades had been led to believe lay in store for them. Before moving in to the area, they were told that it was 'nice and quiet' and that they were going there for a rest.

Finally, 'the shattered remnants of the 13th and 15th Brigades were withdrawn', and the battle came to an end.[22] After many rumours of where they would be moved, the division received orders to proceed to the Somme area to relieve the French. They entrained during the last days of July and early August, and turned their 'backs on Ypres without regret'.

5

The Somme

The battalion remained on the Somme for a number of months. During this time, other than the odd mine explosion and some intermittent shelling and localised minor bombing actions, nothing of specific note occurred within their vicinity. The battalion considered it very quiet and found it a pleasant change from their trying time at Ypres.

There had been thunderstorms and the front-line trenches were in a dreadful state and generally considered to be more of a bother than the enemy. Communication trenches were even worse and were described as being in a 'deplorable state'. Movement would prove, on occasion, to be almost impossible, and any man attempting to travel through the communications trenches usually found himself 'very late, very tired [and] covered with mud'.[1]

August, and a good portion of September, was spent away from the trenches in billets and in Brigade Reserve. The usual rotation in and out of the line continued through the year.

One point of particular note was an extremely successful trench raid, carried out on the night of 6–7 December 1915, 'south of Mametz', involving some three officers and fifty men. A good understanding of enemy conditions was obtained in the raid, and a large number of enemy soldiers killed and captured while Cheshire casualties consisted of two officers slightly wounded, one man mortally wounded, and a further five men slightly wounded. Casualties may have been more severe had the men not been wearing the newly introduced steel helmets that 'proved serviceable' in the raid. These helmets would soon phase out the soft cap worn by men at the front.

Todger was granted a period of leave in December, but he failed to keep to the authorised duration, overstaying his leave by four days over the Christmas period—which also happened to be his birthday—before returning to face the consequences. He was deducted pay and given four days' field punishment (No. 1) for his sins. This was a detested form of punishment and was a cause of much embarrassment for those who endured it.

Pte Bell, of the Army Cycle Corps, describes:

> First Field Punishment was no joke. It meant that you had to parade in full pack and go up and down the road at the double. Everything was done at the double. About turn, left, right, left, right, about turn, left, right, left, right. It was all done under the Military Police and it was hard going, because you had a full pack, tin helmet and all your stuff, sweating up and down the road. Then you took your pack off and it was up against the wagon wheel. They marched me into a field twice a day I was strapped up against the wagon wheel of a General Service limber for an hour in the morning and an hour at night.... It was such a disgrace and it was terrible being strapped to the wheel of the limber. It wasn't so much that it was uncomfortable, though you did get hot and cramped, but I just felt such a proper poppy show. All the chaps looking at you. You really felt the disgrace.[2]

Another soldier gave a similarly negative description:

> Now Field Punishment can be a very nasty thing. In its most extreme form, a man can be tied up to a gun carriage, which isn't at all a pleasant thing. But normally he's sent to what is known as a Field Punishment Barracks, and there the prisoners are tied up for three nights out of four. They're tied up maybe on a fence, or to ropes, with their arms extended and their feet tied together, or they may be tied back to back. It varies in form. And that's done for two hours. Not exactly a pleasant experience.[3]

The field punishment meted out to Todger ended what had been a sombre last couple of months of the year.

Todger's younger brother, Edward Arthur Jones (known as Arthur), was a member of the 10th Cheshires. Prior to the war, he was employed by the Manchester Ship Canal Company but had enlisted on its outbreak with a number his friends, most of whom worked in a local Runcorn tannery. Arthur was a keen cricketer and, like Todger, was well-known socially around the town.

The 10th Cheshires had been formed in September 1914 in Chester and had landed in France towards the end of September the following year. After disembarking, the battalion had endured an eight-hour train journey before being allotted to billets in Strazeele where they remained for several days. Steps had then been put in place for the men to have their first experience of front-line duty. The introduction was gradual, with two or three platoons moving forward each day 'for instruction' and to familiarise themselves with the trenches.[4] Due to this method of duty, the battalion diary is thin on information, as no movement or action was conducted in any strength.

On 6 October, the diary simply states: '3 platoons to Trenches for instruction. Shells fell at GUNNER and LETERNE FARMS. Pte Jones 'B' Coy wounded'.[5] The 'Pte Jones' referred to in the diary was Arthur, who had been shot in the head 'behind the ear' and dangerously wounded by a sniper in what was his first day in the front line. This was in fact his first and last time in the trenches. He would never return to the front. Arthur was moved down the medical staging posts before being shipped home where he would undergo a number of operations to rebuild his skull.

Later that month, on the 25th, Todger had suffered another blow when William Allaby, who was one of his closest friends from Runcorn, lost his life while serving in the Royal Navy as an able seaman onboard HMS *Velox*, a 'torpedo destroyer'. Allaby was killed by an 'explosion' and was forty-seven years old.[6]

Previously, William Allaby had served for an impressive thirty years in the Royal Navy Coastguard. Upon leaving, he had found employment at the Salt Works alongside Todger and the two men had become close drinking buddies.

During his time with the Coastguard, William had distinguished himself on a number of occasions, and his bravery had been formally recognised. In 1911, at Flamborough Head, he had volunteered to be lowered down a cliff by ropes after a man had fallen over the edge. Although unsuccessful, his attempt was said to have posed a great risk of death, prompting his colleagues to present him with a cherry wood pipe and bowl, in which they had placed a gold coin for good luck. He was also issued with a certificate that described him as a 'Carnegie Hero'. It was presented to him by the Carnegie Trust fund together with a cheque for a considerable sum of money, which he refused to cash.[7]

As Todger overstayed his leave and enjoyed Christmas and his birthday in England, the battalion, following a Christmas Day dinner and concert behind the lines, moved into the front-line trenches.

The division moved to the Arras sector in March 1916, where, once again, they were rotated in and out of the line without participating in any major action or set-piece attack. Then, in July, they received orders to return to the Somme. The divisional history concluded: 'Our tour in the Arras area had been a happy one, and we left with regret; both in the line and out of it the time had passed as pleasantly as could be expected'.[8]

The 1916 Somme offensive began on 1 July and consisted of a series of battles lasting until 18 November. Owing to the severity of the casualties inflicted on the attacking troops, the first day of the battle has gone down in history as a dismal failure. Almost 60,000 men would feature on the casualty list, with almost 20,000 of them dead.

The 1st Cheshires played no part in the first-day attacks, and the 5th Battalion was the only one from the regiment to be involved.[9] As pioneers, they were attached in groups to other battalions, accompanying them into the attack with the task of converting the newly captured trenches into defensible positions—

reversing the fire-steps and making them as strong as they could in order to repel any German counterattack. Other tasks included 'bridging trenches' and removing barricades.

After arriving at Mametz on the 19th, the 1st Battalion spent the night in an old German trench on the Pommier Ridge between Mametz and Montauban where they were supplied with extra bombs and small arms ammunition before moving into the support trenches. Over the course of a few days, they dug a new trench to the south-west of Longueval and provided wiring parties and sustained around a score of casualties on a daily basis through enemy artillery. Companies and, in some instances, platoons, began holding sectors of the front line while continuing to provide wiring parties.

The village of Longueval was taken by the division on the 27th, with the Norfolks and Bedfords playing the leading roles in the attack. But the Germans were able to retain a small footing on the northern outskirts, and three parties from the Cheshires, each under an officer, attacked the strongpoints that were holding out. The attack resulted in all three officers being shot, together with many of their men, who attacked through a galling machine-gun fire. The battalion was then relieved, withdrawing into divisional reserve with around 300 men all told.

Todger sent a series of letters home during his time on the Somme. In one, he wrote:

> Our country needs to think well of the men who have undergone the terrible ordeals and privations, undergone daily by our troops and for my part I am glad to think that those in the homeland cannot realise in the least what the Somme battlefield is like. I hope with you that the hordes against us will soon be crushed, and that we may enjoy the peace of home life again. I am sure it will all be a cleaner and more generous race that will spring than those who have tried to rule with mailed fists, and that the world will forever stop any attempt by any nation to prepare armed hordes to the extent our enemy has done.[10]

The battalion received several drafts of reinforcements before taking part in their next action. They moved to Delville Wood before making a number of billet moves while training in skirmishing, night fighting, and also some range shooting for those who were notoriously bad shots. Somewhat worryingly, it was discovered that some of the new arrivals had never thrown a live grenade—a scary prospect since they would be launching an attack within a matter of days where they would be using them in anger. Some hasty training in bomb-throwing took place for the bomb virgins.

Todger himself was a recognised talent when it came to bombing. He was well trained in the tactics that needed to be employed when taking part in bombing fights. The role of the bomber and the tactics used had been considerably refined as the war progressed, so too had the grenades they used. Gone were the days of makeshift projectiles. The Mills bomb had first been issued in May 1915 before production was ramped up. By 1916, it was the general issue grenade among British troops and was in widespread use in all theatres. Prior to that, the British used their creativity in producing effective explosive weaponry. 'We used to save the German stick bombs as far as possible for use against them in an emergency,' wrote Donald Dean, who would earn his own VC in the closing stages of the war, 'but we started making home-made jam-tin-bombs.'[11]

> We saved some of the 1lb jam tins, filled them with a mixture of nails, small scrap or even stones, together with black gunpowder and tied in a detonator into which we inserted a length of fuse. We aimed to use enough fuse to burn for five or six seconds but if we cut off too little the bomb might burst before we got it thrown far enough; if too much fuse then the enemy could throw it back. When we had no tool, the job of crimping the end of the detonator over the end of the fuse, to hold it in place, had to be done with our teeth, not the best of jobs. We then lit the fuse with a match and hoped for the best. A number of small grenade shells were cast by local foundries in France, but the really good hand grenade on which the British Army finally settled was the Mills Bomb. This was heavier than the German egg bomb so they could normally out-throw us, but neither their egg bomb nor their stick bombs had anything like the lethal effect of our Mills. Their stick bombs in particular went off with a much louder bang and could put the wind up inexperienced troops, but I still have several pieces in me, many years afterwards with no ill effect.[12]

Bombing parties were not only integral to the capture of enemy trenches, they also played a crucial part in holding them. The Germans were known for their ability to counterattack, and in losing a position, they would often launch a speedy and ferocious counterstrike. If possible, these usually came from communication trenches linking their lost position with its supports.

After winning a position, the British and their Allied comrades, would quickly set to work with sandbags and anything else close to hand, forming blocks across the trenches, behind which they could defend the position. The importance of doing so was drilled into all bombers, and manuals on grenade parties were circulated to that effect. One manual said: 'In order to hold positions captured from the enemy it is imperative that grenade storming parties hold their final objectives at all costs, and until the positions to be permanently held have been consolidated'.[13]

There was much more to it than simply storming into an enemy trench to exchange grenades with your opposite number. Each man in a bombing squad had his own particular role to carry out. Ideally, a squad would consist of nine men, although in the heat of battle, this was not always possible. Casualties could be inflicted in reaching the trench to begin with and parties could be separated in reaching their objective.

Bombing parties were headed by two bayonet men. These were responsible for protecting the bombers who followed behind them. As the bombers threw their grenades, the lead bayonet man would rush round the traverse immediately after the explosion to deal with any enemy who still had fight left in them. The third and fourth men were the bomb-throwers. These were followed by the leader of the squad who was often an officer but sometimes an NCO. Two bomb carriers were next. These men carried sandbags full of bombs and kept the throwers supplied. Two 'spares' completed the team, one of whom sometimes took to sniping over the traverses or kept watch to ensure the enemy did not leave the trench and launch an attack against them over open ground.

On the morning of 1 September, the Cheshires entered the line at Chimpanzee Trench and Gordon Trench. During an attack by other units two days later, they were told to be prepared to move forward at fifteen minutes' notice. This, they were informed, could occur at any time after 9 a.m. They received the order at 10.20 a.m.

The battalion consulted with the Warwickshires and also the 2nd King's Own Scottish Borderers who had just made an attack, and it quickly became clear that they had suffered very heavily and that the attack had failed. Furthermore, neither battalion seemed 'to be in a position to fully explain the situation' to the Cheshires.[14]

The CO of the KOSB thought that some of his men may have reached their first objective, but he was unsure, and an enemy barrage made it impossible to confirm. A message was sent back to the brigadier explaining the obscurity of the situation and definitive instructions on what to do were requested. A reply was received ordering the Cheshires to send forward some patrols to ascertain the situation.

At 4.25 p.m., word came back that the enemy were retiring. In response, more men were sent forward. Half an hour later, another message was received saying that the enemy were in fact 'reinforcing with a considerable number of troops', and not retiring after all.[15] Brigade received the starling word that 5,000 enemy soldiers were moving up to support their line. By 5.40 p.m., the Cheshires had two companies holding the front line with another in support, while the fourth supported the West Kents holding the front line on the left. Twenty minutes later, another contradictory message was received: '... enemy reinforcements are 50 and not 5,000 as originally stated'.[16] This news was relayed to brigade who then ordered the Cheshires to attack. Orders were issued to 'D' Company at 6.05 p.m., instructing them to attack the trenches to the left of Falfemont Farm at 6.30 p.m. The battalion war diary records:

> 6.30pm: 2nd Lt. A Gwynne-Jones came to Battln. Hdqrs and reported that he had been out on patrol to FALFEMONT FARM and had just returned.

He had got right up to the German wire and under it and found the farm still strongly held by the enemy, and reported accordingly to Brigade.

6.35pm: OC 'D' Company reports failure of attack, being stopped by cross machine gun fire. Owing to the weakness of the Battalion at this time with 1 Company away, OC 16th Royal Warwicks undertook the right part of the attack, and attacked when we did, and also failed.

Casualties very heavy.[17]

In a matter of minutes, 300 men of the battalion had fallen.

For the rest of the day and through the night, attempts were made to organise and find out who was where. Men from various regiments, battalions, and companies were found to be mixed together, and it would be many hours before any semblance of order was restored—and then there were the casualties. Todger's best friend was a battalion stretcher-bearer by the name of Samuel Poxon, whose nickname was 'Poggy'. Poggy was a fearless individual and was known through the battalion for his insistence of going into action in the attacking waves instead of following up behind them. He worked tirelessly in the retrieval of the wounded, showing little concern for danger in his mission to save his comrades. Todger thought the world of Poxon, and the two men shared a close bond.

Shortly after 1 a.m., 'A' Company returned from the West Kents to whom they had been lent. They reported to Brigade HQ in Hardecourt Crucifix where they were informed that another attack was to be launched, and that they would be leading it.

The following afternoon, at 3.10 p.m., they went over the top. The author of the battalion war diary recorded that 'the assaulting company went forward excellently'.[18]

Todger would call it 'a terrific struggle', moving through machine-gun fire against a position that had repulsed four previous attacks. 'Our company had to take the lead at the fifth charge,' Todger later explained. 'The bombers won through and leapt into the trench. We knocked the machine-gunners over and helped the following waves to get through with little loss. It was a terrible journey—the worst, I believe, that I have been through.'[19] The bombers, who attacked with the support of the Bedford's, were led by 2Lt Allan Gwynne-Jones, who received the DSO for the attack.[20]

It would seem that Todger was acting as a lead bayonet man. Either that or he simply found himself at the head of the party as they began to fight their way through the German trench:

> I had a wild three minutes, a rare good do. We got rid of those about us, and I rushed into the next traverse and met my man, a fine big chap, full of fight, a commander of the swell crowd, the First Prussian Guards. He made for me

> with bayonet, but I knew too many tricks even for a Prussian Guard, and I soon settled him.[21]

Todger described seeing a small box fall from the Prussian officer's pocket as he dropped to the ground. On picking it up and opening it, Todger discovered a brand-new, unworn Iron Cross.

Like many a soldier, Todger had a keen interest in souvenirs. His habit had almost gotten him killed at least once, when he was fired at while rummaging through the pockets of dead German soldiers. Whether or not the Iron Cross conveniently 'fell' from his adversary's pocket, as described by Todger, or if it was found by other means, is perhaps open to debate. Whatever the case, the Iron Cross became a treasured possession of Todger's, and every time he looked at it, he was reminded of the one-on-one duel with his opponent who he defeated in what he called a 'fair fight'.

Reinforcements helped to secure the position before a further advance of 3,000 yards past Guillemont was made. They then dug in, too exhausted to go any farther.

The Germans had clung on stubbornly and whole machine-gun detachments had held out to the last until killed at their posts. When the battalion was relieved the following morning, just 280 men walked out of the line.

Once again, Sam Poxon had been performing miracles in rescuing the wounded. Miraculously, he remained untouched, and so too did Todger, but the latter's luck finally ran out as they entered into the support line some 600 yards behind their newly won front, where the enemy were putting down a barrage:

> A party was lost, and I told them I would take them down for a drink, as they had been without food and water for over sixty hours. I got them to the place they had to stay at, got the water, and was making back when one of the big shells plumped alongside me and lifted me about ten yards, a piece getting me in the right shoulder and leg.[22]

Todger was patched up and was set to be shunted down the line with the other casualties. But he turned his nose up at the chance of respite and opted to return to his unit instead:

> I refused to go down the line, and though my arm was useless for a day or two, and was a bit stiff and painful when I won the V.C., it was all a streak of luck, for if I'd gone to hospital I should have missed the funniest round-up I've ever seen.[23]

The round-up he was referring to was of course his capture of over 100 German soldiers, which was about to take place in the very near future.

6

'I Laughed like Blazes'

On 25 September, as part of a large offensive launched along a 6-mile front on the Somme, the battalion assaulted the village of Morval.

As far as the Cheshires were concerned, the Bedfords were heading the attack within their own brigade, which was attacking on a one-battalion front. Their attack consisted of distinct stages, the first being the capture of the German front line at the bottom of a valley between Ginchy and Morval. The next objective was given to the Norfolks, who were to attack up the slopes of Morval and take the support line. Lastly, the Cheshires would pass through to capture the eastern edge of Morval itself. The final objective—'a line from which observation could be obtained on Sailly-Saillisel and Le Transloy'—was given to the Warwickshires.

The attack on Morval was well co-ordinated and a great success. At 12.55 p.m., the Norfolks captured their objective. They were closely followed by the Bedfords and Cheshires, who, at 2.42 p.m., under a perfect creeping barrage, reached the western edge of Morval. They pushed rapidly through the village itself, and just twelve minutes later had reached its eastern outskirts.

The Cheshires's war diary summed up the success:

> The features of the attack were that each assaulting wave left its trench exactly in accordance with Operation Orders, artillery barrages were excellent and objectives were taken in every case at the first assault. Our casualties were not very heavy and MORVAL was taken by the battalion at about 3 p.m.[1]

Once the initial resistance had been broken, the enemy were swiftly swept aside, and many prisoners were taken. The Germans, it seemed, were thoroughly disorganised. Nevertheless, they remained nearby in large numbers.

With Morval secured, efforts were immediately made to dig in and entrench along its outskirts. To the east of the village, close to where the Cheshires were in the process of consolidating, an old network of German 'practice' trenches existed. These, it was soon discovered, held an unknown number of enemy soldiers—including snipers, who proceeded to fire on the parties of Cheshire men who were busy digging. This fire, described as causing 'much annoyance to the troops consolidating', provoked Todger to carry out a daring and risky proactive response.

The divisional history, after noting the snipers' fire, went on to record:

> This led to an astonishing exploit: crawling out to one of these trenches alone, Private Jones, of the Cheshires, captured single-handed 200 Germans and led them in triumph back to our lines, and act for which he was awarded the V.C.[2]

The divisional history is not quite correct in its finer detail—the number of prisoners that Todger actually secured being below the quoted figure. It was, nevertheless, 'an astonishing exploit'.

The Victoria Cross

Todger was busy with his shovel as the enemy snipers started firing. While some bullets zipped harmlessly past, others struck flesh and bone, and men began to drop. At first, Todger was frustrated, but as more casualties were inflicted, this frustration turned to anger. Todger asked his officer for permission to 'have a go' at them, but the officer refused, explaining that his orders were to consolidate as quickly as possible in case of a counterattack, and that no time could be wasted.

The snipers, however, continued to pick off the diggers. A man, who at the time was stood behind Todger waiting his turn on the shovel, was then hit. Glancing across towards the German position, Todger saw what he took to be a white flag. This flag coupled with the incoming rifle fire filled Todger with rage. Pointing it out to his officer, Todger asked him what he thought of it. His question was met with the same abrupt response—'carry on with your digging!'

The final straw is said to have been when a young private by the name of George Kenworthy was killed after being shot through the head. The story goes that it was Kenworthy's eighteenth birthday and that he was in the process of explaining this to Todger as the shot rang out.[3]

The origins of this widely circulated story are not entirely clear, but a similar story was brought up at a reunion many years later, shortly before Todger's death, where it was reported:

> A runner in the Battalion had just said he was 18 that day, and had promised Todger a feed and a drink later that day, when an enemy bullet killed him.
>
> 'Todger's' unthinking reaction was to 'get the chaps that did it', and he ran for the enemy lines.[4]

Kenworthy was indeed killed that day, but he was not eighteen years old; he was twenty-two, and a regular soldier, having enlisted just two weeks prior to the commencement of war in 1914, aged nineteen.[5]

Kenworthy had returned to the battalion just six days before his death after being wounded during their attack on Falfemont Farm earlier in the month. The wound—a gunshot to the nose—had not been too severe, but it had been sufficient enough to keep him away from the battalion for two weeks.

Todger, who did not mention Kenworthy in any of his subsequent accounts, described the event that caused him to throw down his entrenching tool and snatch up his rifle:

> I felt the bullets ping-pinging by me and I said to the officer, 'they're going to make it hot for us, Sir, if we don't get after 'em. Can I get out and have a packet at them?'
>
> 'My orders are to consolidate this position,' replied the officer. 'You must not go an inch farther, and you had better get on with your digging.'
>
> And dig I did, but as I got up again I saw a chap hit through the head and another through the thigh. Looking ahead, I saw what appeared to be a white flag, and that fairly riled me. My 'dander' was up and I shouted to the officer, 'what do you think of that Sir?'
>
> 'You must get on with your digging, Jones,' said he; but up I jumped and called out 'If I've got to be killed, I'll die fighting, not digging.'[6]

After slinging down his entrenching tool, Todger picked up his rifle, 'jumped out of the trench and went across'.[7]

Quite what he was expecting to achieve is not clear, and in all likelihood, he did not actually know himself. The red mist had descended, and in a fit of rage and frustration, no doubt coupled with large amounts of adrenaline, Todger had begun what was essentially a one-man assault, launched on the spur of the moment against a position 150–200 yards away, against an enemy whose strength was completely unknown.

Todger's comrades watched in both amazement and horror as he ran off without warning. One man of the battalion, a sergeant, said that the barrage was very heavy at the place he was going and 'the lads thought it was the last of him.... We watched every second expecting to see him go down.'[8]

But Todger did not 'go down'. He made it to the enemy trench, leapt in, and disappeared from sight. As they lost sight of him, a comrade watching from across the way uttered to his friends, 'poor old man.' It was assumed by all that Todger would soon be dead.[9]

Todger's journey across no-man's-land was an ordeal in itself. The fatal shot did not come, nor did any of the thousands of lumps of shrapnel find its mark as he made his way across, but there were several lucky escapes along the way.

Sniper fire tore up chunks of dirt as the bullets struck the ground around him. One bullet crashed into his helmet, piercing the front. It spun round the inside before becoming 'spent' and exiting down his back. It was a lucky escape.

Further bullets pierced his clothing, but Todger remained unhurt. After noticing a sniper firing at him from a tree, Todger returned fire and picked off his opponent before continuing to push on. According to his citation, two others 'who were displaying a white flag' were also shot dead.

As he got near, Todger's instincts as a bomber came into play, and he made his approach with precision as per the training manual, deliberately angling his line of advance by approaching the German trench from the flank. This ensured that any enemy soldiers within it could only come at him from one side.

Three Germans quickly set upon Todger as he entered the trench:

> I had only one at a time to deal with. I got my back to the wall, and they whipped round on me. I always believe in firing from the hip and very quickly number one dropped dead. Before the next man could recover his senses I had shot him as well, slipped another cartridge in the breech and got the old magazine going on the third at a yard range.[10]

His one-man attack continued into the next bay, where more enemy soldiers were encountered:

> In the second traverse there were five chaps standing behind one another. One of them made for me with his bayonet, but I bowled him over like the others by the old trick of shooting from the hip. I got the five of them...[11]

Todger never did explain how he managed to single-handedly defeat five enemy soldiers, although he did later explain that 'some of them made awful noises, screaming and squealing' as he killed them.[12]

By now, he had worked himself up into a frenzy. He shouted and screamed at the top of his lungs as he dashed round the traverses in search of more Germans to kill. Most, however, had bolted into their dugouts at the sound of fighting, no doubt surmising they were under attack by something more than a lone private who had simply lost his temper.

Todger halted when he came upon a dugout that was one of a series in the area. A German soldier lingering at the entrance fired a quick and panicked shot that missed its target before turning and bolting down the steps. Todger caught sight of several other figures moving around in the dugout and heard 'shouting and screeching' as he fired down at them. Things then went quiet. Todger had a quick look around at the contents of the trench and was pleased to find a stock of grenades among the equipment that was strewn about. He grabbed them and began hurling them into the nearest dugout. 'I think they felt the game was up when the bombs began to drop amongst them,' Todger related, 'for up rushed three fine specimens with their hands up and the usual cry "Mercy, *Kamarad*!"'[13]

> They had left equipment behind them to show there was no 'monkeying' and though I felt like laughing at being there all on my own, I demanded in a stern voice if any one of them could speak English. One of them called out 'I can'.
>
> 'Well,' said I, 'what is it to be? Do you want to be killed or taken prisoners? You can have it either way you like, for I am not particular. In fact, I would rather kill you.'
>
> And all with one consent actually cried out that they wanted to become prisoners and with Private Jones as their jailer, too![14]

Looking round, Todger spotted a large hollow that he decided to use as a compound to hold his prisoners. It was an ideal spot that he could easily observe. Also, the Germans would have to scale the trench and climb down the other side to get into it and Todger hoped his comrades would see what was happening and come to his aid.

Todger ordered two of the three prisoners into the hollow before turning to the English-speaker:

> 'How many more are there down the dug-out?' I asked, and the Boche answered 'about fifteen'.
>
> 'What about it?' I said, and he replied 'what do you mean?'
>
> 'Do they want killing or what?' said I, and he gasped, 'I don't know.'
>
> 'Well then,' said I, 'go and tell them what I have told you—that they can either be killed or taken prisoners and they can bloomin' well please themselves about it.'
>
> And by gum! He went and told them and came back to say they would all be taken prisoners.[15]

Todger instructed the English-speaker to tell those in the dugout to come out one by one, 'and no rushing'. He made it clear that any man seen to be holding a weapon would be instantly shot.[16]

As a further precaution, realising the vulnerability of his position, Todger then performed what can only be described as a magnificent bluff. He informed them through his interpreter that his 'mates' were coming across in their thousands any minute, and if they found anything wrong with him, they would be 'cut to bits'.[17]

The men of the first dugout emerged and moved into the hollow without incident. There were other dugouts nearby, and heads were soon peeking out at the commotion.

The surrender of those in the first dugout had a ripple effect, and those in the other dugouts soon began to leave their sanctuaries with their hands above their heads.

> Lord! I'd expected fifteen and out they came in scores and went in my 'compound'. When they were all out, I threw some of their own bombs into the dug-outs to make sure that there was no sniper left behind to 'do me in'. And then I said to myself 'Great Scot! What am I going to do with this little lot?'[18]

Todger now had somewhere in the region of 150 Germans in his hollow. He was still hopeful that his comrades would come across to back him up but, as yet, nobody had come. He was playing a lone hand.

In order to stall things, Todger concocted a plan, which he disguised as an act of good will:

> It's not that I want to brag, but I didn't turn a hair; I just kept my head-piece going. I told them it would be a very cold night at the place where they were going to, and suggested they had better get their great-coats. I graciously permitted them to fetch them 'two at a time, and no rushing.'
>
> They ran and came in and out, and each time they passed me they saluted me, Private Jones!—and I sent them to their places. I didn't like the look of one 'bloke' and kept half an eye on him.
>
> 'I think I'll shoot that chap,' I said to the interpreter.
>
> 'Don't,' he exclaimed, 'he very good man.'
>
> But presently the 'very good man' went for his great-coat and when he had got a short distance he made a dash for liberty. I swung round, clicked my rifle and got him fair and square. He rolled over and over just like a rabbit. It was a snap-shot, but I put one through his head. Then I turned to the German by me.
>
> 'Ask them if any more would like to try to escape,' I said.
>
> He did so, and they all jumped up—they were seated on the ground—flinging up their arms and shouted '*Kamarad*!' It fairly tickled me to death that did and I couldn't stop laughing.[19]

Todger later said that the sight of the Germans with their hands up reminded him of a pantomime that he had seen, and it was this that had brought on his spontaneous fit of laughter.

In the pantomime, a squire had rounded up all the 'servants, male and female, butlers and gardeners' and coerced them into surrender by pointing a gun at them. They had all flung up their hands. The squire had then pointed his weapon at the grandfather clock, and that too had flung up its hands—or rather the two 'hands' on the clock face. 'Well, I tell you I roared with laughter at the thought coming into my mind at such a time, when I was playing a lone hand,' Todger explained, 'for it looked so comical to see them all with their hands up—over a hundred of 'em—hoping against hope that Private Jones, *Kamarad*, wouldn't shoot.'[20]

After calming down somewhat from the amusing scene, Todger peered back across no-man's-land to see a man just starting from the British line. Todger breathed a huge sigh of relief at the sight of this as-yet unknown individual coming to back him up. As he got nearer, Todger recognised the man. It was Sam Poxon—his best friend.

At first, Poggy had not been aware that Todger had gone over the top by himself. He only learnt of it after moving up to those who were digging in, perhaps to treat those who had been hit. Realising Todger was not there, Poggy had asked about Todger's whereabouts and was subsequently informed about what had happened. He was told that Todger was probably dead, but Poggy did not hesitate in going to find him, telling the men: 'If Todger's across there, I'm going to fetch him, dead or alive!'[21]

He had then jumped out of the trench and ran across. Another stretcher-bearer followed his lead and went after him; so too did a sergeant-major and another man whose identity is not known.

Todger related:

> My heart went up when I saw Poxon coming. It were grand to see him! He first gave me a clout on the ear. That was his way of greeting me. I said, 'What do you think of this lot, Sammy?'[22]

The two men shared a laugh and Poggy made a remark about there being some very good souvenirs among the captives.

The prisoners were rounded up and Todger, with the help of his comrades began to walk them back to their own lines. Leading them triumphantly from the front, Todger received rousing cheers from the British line as they saw him bringing them back. Various officers from the flanking units who had seen the entire episode unfold through their field glasses would later make enquiries as to the identity of the man who achieved it.

Officially, the number of prisoners was recorded as 102. Todger, however, thought the number was originally closer to 150—he estimates even higher than this in one account—but some had been lost on the way back, owing to a British barrage that was landing in no-man's-land. Todger picked up another slight wound in this barrage, but once again fortune favoured the brave, and he escaped with nothing more than a graze from a glancing piece of shrapnel

It was not until his return that Todger noticed several holes in his tunic. He also checked his helmet and discovered that it was heavily dented with a bullet hole in the front from the sniper who had shot at him when he was going across.

Todger was ordered to personally take his prisoners back behind the lines. He did so, marching some 4–5 miles before handing them over.

Despite the nature of the ordeal, it would seem Todger was not overly concerned about his near-death experience:

> Looking back and thinking over the incident, I feel that I must have had what the poets call 'a charmed life', for, after jumping out of the trench and

> before I had accounted for the sniper in the tree, a bullet went through my helmet and was buzzing round my head-piece like a marble in a basin, finally galloping down my back and burning me during the journey. Four or five other bullets passed through my tunic, but I wasn't aware of it until afterwards. It never entered my mind that I should be killed and I didn't think my time had come.[23]

The day ended with complete success. Battalion HQ had been positioned further back at Quadrilateral Trench when the battle had commenced, and they had seen the attack on Morval develop. Long before receiving word of the success, they could tell the battalion had captured its objective. At about 5 p.m., Battalion HQ moved forward to a sunken road west of Morval, while the CO moved into Morval itself where it was recorded that, other than heavy shelling, the situation was now quiet.

The war diary concluded for the day:

> A tremendous number of prisoners were taken and these kept coming in the whole evening, and the reports from the Companies showed that the Germans in front were entirely disorganised.
>
> In the evening and throughout the night the Germans shelled MORVAL very heavily, and also trenches in front of MORVAL.[24]

Thousands of enemy soldiers had been captured through the day and those who were involved in the attack received several congratulatory messages from the higher echelons.

Army Commander Gen. Sir H. Rawlinson gave particular praise to the Cheshire Regiment's 5th Division:

> Please convey to Guards, 6th, 5th and 56th Divisions my thanks for and admiration of the excellent manner in which they carried out their attacks to-day. Special credit is due to 5th Division who have already undertaken two prolonged and successful offensives since July 20th.[25]

A direct message to the division was also received:

> The G.O.C. wishes to thanks all ranks in the Division for their magnificent conduct yesterday.
>
> In spite of their heavy losses in previous actions and the hardships which they have endued during the recent bad weather they have shown that their spirit is as good as ever.
>
> No task is too hard for the 5th Division.
>
> General Staff, 5th Division.[26]

The Fifth Division in the Great War's assessment describes them in similar glowing terms:

> The heavy fighting in Delville Wood and Longueval, the attack and capture of the Falfemont Farm Line and Leuze Wood, and finally the storming of Morval, are feats of arms seldom equalled in the annals of the British Army. They constitute a record of unvarying success which it has been the lot of few Divisions to attain, and the gallantry, valour, and endurance of all ranks have been wholly admirable.'[27]

7

Heartiest Congratulations

All thought of what he had achieved that day at Morval had soon vanished from Todger's mind. In a letter to his mother written shortly after the event, he had explained that his wound—the one sustained by enemy shellfire at the beginning of the month after the Falfemont Farm action—was coming along well. He also provided a somewhat simplified and modest version of what had happened at Morval on the 25th:

> My wound is nearly better, it was in the shoulder and I would not leave the battalion. I have been in action twice since, and God again has cared for me and got me through all dangers. It seems as thought your prayers for my safety have been more than answered.
>
> We had taken a position and were taking another when I felt a bullet passing me. I knew they would get me if something was not done, so I went across. While going one bullet passed through my steel helmet and four more through my jacket.
>
> When I got through I soon settled them. Some of them shouted at me from their dug-out entrances until I settled accounts with them. The rest was easy.
>
> They started flinging their arms up, and I soon got the fear of God in them. Two of my chums got across and helped to get them away to our lines. We took 100 back with us.
>
> I got a shrapnel wound in the neck in our barrage, it was not much and is alright now.[1]

Todger was unaware that word of his achievement was rapidly working its way up the chain of command and several officers were in the process of writing up their recommendations for the award of the VC.

Towards the end of October, when Todger did get wind of the award, it occurred in somewhat humorous circumstances. 'Well I had completely forgotten it,' said Todger, 'when a chap came to me and said "Have you a Victoria Cross?"'

> I said 'No, but I've an Iron Cross here I'll sell if you're trading.'
> 'Well', the chap said, 'No I don't mean that.'
> 'What are you getting at?' I asked, 'Are you potty, hop it my lad' and I left him.[2]

If Todger was baffled by this strange encounter, his confusion was further heightened by what followed:

> I was then met by a Sergeant who said, 'Put it there, my lad' holding out his hand. I said, 'What's up with you all this morning?' and he replied 'It's alright, my lad, I am right glad to shake hands with you.'
>
> Well, I went on to the transport Sergeant and asked if there was any mail and he came over to me and said, 'Put it there young fellow, and best of luck with you' holding out his hand.
>
> 'Look here' I said. 'Will you tell me what's the matter with you all this morning?'[3]

The transport sergeant handed Todger a telegram addressed to him from regimental depot at 'The Castle' in England. It read: 'Heartiest congratulations from all ranks at the depot, Chester'.[4] Todger then realised that 'something was up'. This was soon confirmed when he received a notification from headquarters telling him he had been awarded the VC.

News of the award reached Runcorn about the same time. On 26 October, Pte Findlow, who was a member of the military staff, was sent from Chester Castle by the officers of the Cheshire Regiment to break the news to Todger's parents. This was later followed up by a message from the Records Office at Shrewsbury.

The details of what Todger had done were somewhat vague at this time. The day after the news had broke, an article in the local *Runcorn Guardian* explained a little about the kind of man Todger was:

> To the many Runcornians who know Jones the news was a great pleasure without being a surprise. Most of them regarded the recipient as belonging to the type of men who show great personal coolness and courage in positions of danger. In addition, it was generally known that Private Jones had already distinguished himself by daring deeds, and had been somewhat unfortunate inasmuch as several officers who had noted his courage and informed him that he would be recommended for honours were killed before the opportunity of doing so arose.[5]

Upon hearing the news, Mr Alfred Dodd, 'who has known Private Jones intimately for many years', said of Todger:

> Private Jones is of rather spare build, of medium height, and of a cold, phlegmatic temperament, which makes him an ideal soldier for trench warfare so much in evidence at the present time. He has always been known among his companions for his cool temperament and his sangfroid in all sorts of disturbing circumstances. He has always been very popular among his workmates and companions, and has taken an active part in athletics of every description. From an early age he had a passion for soldiering, which led him early in life to enlist in the Volunteers, and later the Territorials. He has always won eulogies from his officers for smartness, and especially for his marksmanship, having carried off several first-class prizes, often in competition with men older and more experienced.... There is no doubt that Private Jones would have attained distinction earlier but for the continued misfortune he had in having his officers, who had promised to recommend him for distinction, killed, with the result that the recommendations for his gallantry could not be forwarded to the proper quarters.[6]

Soon, through various channels, including letters from comrades detailing what had happened, word of what Todger had achieved became well known. His parents were inundated with letters of congratulation on their son having been awarded the coveted cross. Todger's mother received one from Maj. Ashton, who had formerly commanded the Runcorn Volunteers when Todger was serving with them and who was now serving at the front.

Ashton wrote:

> Dear Mrs Jones,
>
> I have received from Major Timmins a newspaper cutting describing the wonderful bravery of your son, for which he has received the V.C. Runcorn will feel justly proud of being able to claim a man who has done one of the most remarkable deeds of the war as a townsfolk. Personally I feel a special pride and delight in the fact that he is an old Runcorn Volunteer, and served at a time when I was in command. I trust that his glorious accomplishment will be recorded on the walls of the Drill Hall as an incentive to brave actions by other men of the present and future generations. You must be a very proud mother, and I congratulate you on having such a son.[7]

The town went wild as they heard about Todger's VC. The street where he lived was decorated with bunting from top to bottom, and the townsfolk partied in celebration.

The '*Boy's Own*' nature of the deed furthered the jubilation. Ultimately, his story did feature in the *Boy's Own* publication, as well as national newspapers up and down the country.

The Cheshire Regiment journal, *The Oak Tree*, also ran a story about Todger's heroics. It gave the readers further information about Todger as a man, and how he had excelled in other ways since his arrival on the Western Front:

> 'Todger' as his pals call him, has throughout his time at the front shown in endless instances a devil-may-care contempt for danger, and has performed very many acts of gallantry.
>
> His 'drumming up' for the men of the Company while under a hot fire from the Hun trenches is one instance of his coolness. Owing to a mishap to his own rifle he made teas and took it round to buck them up. Somehow he always succeeded in having a fire on which to cook anything that was going.
>
> On another occasion, at night, about 50 men of another Regiment had lost their way under a heavy fire. Jones happened to be returning from the trenches, he met those 50 men and guided them into safety. He was always cheerful and happy, and by his good spirits kept the men lively.
>
> His letter to his mother describing the act which gained him his V.C. is quite devoid of 'swank'. It reads as if he had thoroughly enjoyed himself. 'Some of the Germans shot at me from their dugout entrance,' he wrote, 'until I settled accounts with them.' The rest was easy. They flung up their arms as soon as I got near them, as I put the fear of God into them.' This sounds simple enough, but one can imagine the 'settling' before 'the rest became easy' was what did put the fear of God into them!'[8]

On 3 November 1916, the *Runcorn Weekly News* reported:

> Since the receipt of the news that their son has been granted the Victoria Cross, Mr & Mrs Jones, of Princess Street, have been overwhelmed by messages of congratulations, verbal, and by letter and wire. When Private Thomas Alfred Jones obtains the leave to which so many people are looking forward, he may, should he chose to, spend a few hours answering communication expressing the hearty good wishes of relatives and friends, even of persons who have no acquaintance with him but appreciate his gallant deeds. Meanwhile Runcorn feels deeply the date of the hero's return. Rumours were circulated in the town on Tuesday to the effect that he was due home immediately, but none were based on fact. The only communication his parents have had from him since the announcement of the award was a field card on Tuesday morning, stating he was quite well and was writing further.[9]

Todger was granted his highly anticipated leave later that month. He arrived in London from the Western Front before travelling on the last leg of his journey from Euston to Runcorn.

Several other Runcorn men were on the train. Pte Leonard Pollit of the 5th Battalion Cheshire Regiment was one of them. Pollit, who resided in Rutland

Street near to where Todger lived, had also been decorated for his bravery. In April 1915 at Ypres, Pollit had made a spirited dash into no-man's-land under heavy fire to rescue an officer and two men. One of the men was his friend and fellow Runcorn man, Sgt Nichols. Politt had carried Nichols on his back to safety and had received two bullet holes through his cap—one of which had grazed his face—in the process. His actions, and the fact that he got through without serious injury, were quite remarkable and had resulted in the award of the Distinguished Conduct Medal (DCM). His medal was the first of its kind to be awarded to the battalion.[10] Pollit had been presented with his medal in the field by Gen. Maude, and he was now on the way home for a well-earned period of leave, although his homecoming would prove to be somewhat overshadowed by the scenes that awaited Todger.

At Euston, Todger had been recognised by the station-master and a few other members of the station staff, who had asked if they could do anything for him. Owing to Todger keeping his head down, the train journey itself was completed in relative peace, and he was thankful not to be recognised by any fellow passengers or staff.

Back in Runcorn, it was a different matter. The townsfolk had known that Todger was due home sometime soon, but it was believed he would not be leaving France until the 17th. It was now the 9th. Todger was early, and no preparations whatsoever had been made.

From Euston, Todger had fired off a telegram to his parents, telling them he was boarding the 2.55 p.m. train to Runcorn. This was the first notion they had of their son's return from the front. The telegram kick-started frantic and urgent efforts to make worthy arrangements for his imminent homecoming.

As word rapidly spread through the town, drastic action was taken. Schools and workplaces immediately declared a half day's holiday and closed. Schoolchildren flocked the streets, singing patriotic songs and waving flags in celebration. Meanwhile, the entire town knuckled down to put together a last-minute reception.

Just two hours had passed since Todger's telegram had been received. The streets were now completely packed and crowds stretched from the station right through the town to Todger's home. The entire route was lavishly decorated. 'Everyone who possessed a flag brought it out for the occasion,' reported the *Runcorn Guardian*, 'and very soon the main streets were festooned with miles of bunting.'[11]

A brass band was rapidly assembled and rushed to the station. The wounded soldiers who could manage it marched down from the nearby Cottage and Vicarage hospitals to form a guard of honour alongside the Runcorn volunteers under Maj. Timmins.

Meanwhile, Todger's train neared its destination. Earlier, two of his nephews had jumped a train to Crewe, further down the line from Runcorn.

From Crewe, they detrained and boarded Todger's train as it came into the station. Handshakes, smiles, and a patting of the back took place when they linked up with him, but they made no mention of what awaited their uncle back home. As they completed the final stretch of the journey, Todger remained completely ignorant of what lay in store. What waited was the biggest turnout in the streets of Runcorn since the coronation of George V.[12]

Todger's heart sank when the train pulled into the station. He had expected a normal and uneventful return. Instead, a lavish ceremony awaited. Thousands of residents were screaming and waving flags as the train pulled in. Todger was both astounded and horrified.

His parents stood on the head of the platform, beaming with pride, eagerly awaiting the arrival of their son. Local council leaders and various other dignitaries stood alongside them, as did his brothers and sisters.

Amid rousing cheers, Todger, who was sat in one of the front carriages of the train, was almost dragged out by his friends. He was soon embracing his mother and then his father. One of the first questions Pte Jones asked was 'What's all the fuss about?'[13]

Todger later confessed that he only expected to see his relatives and a few close friends at the station, and if he had known what awaited him, he would have gone on a different line and headed to Manchester, and from there to Runcorn's neighbouring town of Widnes. He also stated that he would almost as soon go back to the front than face what awaited him back home.

After a brief stay in the general waiting room that had been reserved for him by the station officials, Todger made his way to the other platform, followed by his brother who carried his kitbag and also his steel helmet that boasted a large dint and bullet hole from the sniper.

With the initial greetings over, an embarrassed Pte Jones set out to try and get home. The crowd screamed with excitement, and progress was slow as he tried to fight his way through them. Many people reached out to shake his hand, and those that could not simply touched him.

In the words of the *Chester Chronicle*:

> Private Jones went through the ordeal of shaking hands with hundreds of admirers. Many of them were school children, whose faces beamed sunshine with the satisfaction of having personally welcomed home a hero whose deeds have become known throughout the land.[14]

After a short while, with the chairman and vice-chairman of the local council alongside him, Todger was hoisted up and carried shoulder high part of the way home. Further along, at his own request, he was lowered to the ground on to his own two feet.

In Devonshire Square, in the centre of the town, the chairman of the council, from the footboard of the car containing the Jones family, delivered a short speech. Then, as Todger neared his home, he took drastic measures to evade the baying mobs: 'In Devonshire Street, the principal thoroughfare, progress was impossible, and finally Jones took to his heels down a side street to his home, arriving almost exhausted'.[15]

In describing Todger's difficult journey home, the *Runcorn Guardian* wrote:

> A somewhat amusing incident followed. It was clearly hopeless for Jones to attempt to get to his house via the Square and Regent Street. The car suddenly swerved down High-street, Private Jones leaped out and nimbly ran into Back High Street and to his parents' house by the back passage.[16]

This incident would become a well-known and humorous story and Todger would be constantly reminded of it for years to come.

Todger escaped the crowds, ran to his parent's house, and slammed the door behind him, but the sanctuary of home did little to disperse the numbers. Hundreds of people filled the street outside his home hoping to get a glimpse of their local hero. It took half a dozen constables to guard the door of his home to stop overexcited members of the public from entering the house. Instead, they stood in the street and shouted for him to re-emerge.

Meanwhile, the Highfield Band played in the street directly in front of the house. Their songs included 'See the Conquering Heron Comes' and 'Rule Britannia'. Eventually, the reluctant hero appeared at the front bedroom window, resulting in a deafening cheer from the eager audience. They shouted for him to say a few words and Todger called on them to give 'three cheers for the lads still in the trenches, and for the wounded soldiers from the local hospital, who had formed a guard of honour for him at the station'.[17]

This deflection of his own actions became a common trait of Todger's. In the interviews that followed, he would often highlight the work of others, giving praise where he felt it was warranted while shying away from speaking about himself or his actions.

Over the course of the next few hours, the crowds began to dwindle until they had all but gone, but visitors continued to knock at the door. A representative from the *Runcorn Guardian* newspaper, who happened to be an old school friend of Todger, waiting patiently outside was eventually let in.

The newspaper published their findings the following day:

> Jones is a genial man, and bore his lionizing with the greatest good humour and modesty. But he admitted that his arm ached badly when he invited the waiting *Guardian* representative into the little parlour of his home, hailing him with genuine pleasure as an old schoolmate.
>
> 'Let's hear all about it, Tom,' was the comprehensive demand made upon him.
>
> 'Righto' was the cheery answer. 'This is all there is to tell. On the 25th September orders were given to us to take a village. We did it and got through

all right. We landed on the edge of a wood and were told to dig in there. We had been digging a minute or two when the bullets started flying around us. I turned to our lieutenant and remarked 'They are going to make it hot for us if we don't get without them, sir. He replied 'You can't go over there. Get on with your digging, Jones.' I said 'All right sir' and went at it with the spade. The bullets started coming again, and the chap behind me got hit in the leg. I had a look over the top and saw what I took to be a white flag being shown. That got my temper up and I said to my officer. 'What do you think about that, sir?' He said what he thought very seriously. I said 'Let's get without them.' He said we had better go on digging, but I remarked 'If I have to be killed I'll die fighting and not digging.' So I jumped up and went across. Of course, they spotted me coming and one bullet went through my steel helmet and three more through my tunic. I got over all right and jumped in the end of the trench. There were three men at the end. I managed to 'get without them' and got my old magazine going on some others. The others rushed into their dug-outs. For a minute or two—which felt like hours to me—they fired at me from the door of the dug-out. I managed to get there first every time, which is the great thing in jobs of this kind.

'At the finish I was by myself. There was not a soul in sight. They had all gone to earth! Our own shell fire, which was terrible at the time, no doubt helped them in their decision.'

'I got hold of some of their bombs and flung them into a dug-out. They were made in Germany but they went of all right. Then three chaps came running out with their hands up. It was the usual thing—'Mercy *kamerad*.' I said, 'What's it got to be? Do you want to be prisoners?' They said, 'Yes, yes! We want to be prisoners.' I said, 'All right: do any of you speak English?' One said, 'Yes: I can speak good English.' I asked, 'Are there any more down there?' He replied, 'About fifteen.' I said 'Tell 'em to come up and be taken prisoner or killed. My mates are coming across in a minute in thousands. If there's anything wrong with me when they come they'll cut you to pieces.' He went and told his comrades what I said. When he returned I asked, 'What do they say?' He replied, 'They are quite willing to come as prisoners.' I said 'Very well. If anyone comes up with arms or equipment he will be shot dead straight away.' He went along and told them and they came tumbling up one by one from the dug-outs—eight or nine dug-outs in all. When they all lined up before me I thought to myself 'Good Lord, what am I going to do with this lot!' But while I stood in front of them I knew someone would come to my help. No British lads leave you to it. I knew they'd come sooner or later.

'To pass the time away and give me a chance I told them it would be very cold at night where they were going to, and they had better get their top coats. I told them to fetch them two men at a time, and they did so. That took up about ten minutes. One fellow, whose looks I didn't like, suddenly made a dash for it. I swung round and took a snap shot at him. It was a lucky one, for it got him right in the 'crust', and he rolled over like a rabbit. 'Is there anyone else wants to escape?' They all flung their hands up. The sight did me good, and I roared with laughter. It looked so comical. I glanced over the top again and saw some chaps starting from our lines. They were four of my pals, and when they came across I was jolly glad to see them. They helped me to round them up, and we got them across all right. I think there was about 180 altogether, including one general staff officer.

'And what sort of reception did you get when you got back?' was the question put to Private Jones.

'Oh, the lads shouted a lot', he replied nonchalantly. 'They thought I'd gone under. Some one said to my pals "Todger's over yonder," and one of them replied. "If he is I'm coming to fetch him back dead or alive." My heart went up when I saw my old pals coming across to me.'[18]

The day after Todger's return, the *Runcorn Weekly News* reported:

Yesterday [Thursday] was the great day in the history of Runcorn, for it witnessed the homecoming of Tom Jones VC the first lad in Runcorn to win the coveted honour as well as the first lad in the Cheshire Regiment. To say that Runcorn was wild with enthusiasm is but to describe the scenes in the mildest possible manner, for the whole town combined in one huge burst of enthusiasm and joyous welcome, and its warmth was all the more marked in as much as the notice of his coming was so short. It was generally anticipated that he would leave France on the 17th, and the arrangements for his reception were being made or about that time. In the middle of Thursday morning, however, a telegram handed in at Euston by Jones himself reached his parents, informing them that he hoped to arrive home by the 2-55 at Runcorn Station.[19]

Later that evening, when things had died down, Todger visited the Liberal Club where he enjoyed a few drinks with his friends and fellow members. That same evening, the Runcorn Urban Council held a scheduled meeting. At the conclusion of business, the chairman, Mr. A. T. Smith, said 'that all members would be aware that a Runcorn man had succeeded in winning the highest honour which it was in the power of the King to give any Englishman—the Victoria Cross.'[20]

Smith went on:

It was a distinction that any man would be proud of. It was open to the highest or the lowest in the land without fear or favour, and was won by valour in the field in the face of England's enemies. The circumstances attended the granting of this particular Victoria Cross were such that not only Runcorn, but the whole nation, would be proud of them. For a man to walk single-handed from our trenches into the German trenches and by sheer impudence collar 102 of

> them was really something to be proud of. To know that it had been done by a Runcorn man added a considerable amount of glory to the act. Everyone knew that Runcorn men were good workers, good fighters and good players, who played the game right through to the end on every occasion.
>
> Runcorn had made her mark in the history of England. It was probably known to many of them that 500 years ago a Runcorn man, Sir John Savage, had carried the standard at the Battle of Agincourt. Recently he saw a wreath of fresh flowers on the effigy of Henry V. in Westminster Abbey, and was reminded of that incident. And now Private Jones had brought a wreath of honour to Runcorn. He was glad to have him as a Runcornian, and all of them were proud of the noble deed he had done.[21]

It was discussed what could be done to acknowledge the VC and what public recognition could be given. It had been hoped to provide Todger with financial reward in the form of a treasury bond or a war saving certificate, but 'owing to the provisions of a recent Army Order, it was impossible to make him a present of money'.[22] This had been banned 'because it was considered a soldier did his duty for the love of the thing' and was not spurred on to perform an act of bravery for the sole purpose of seeking or gaining financial reward.[23]

In the end, it was decided that recognition from the council would come in the form of a gold-inscribed watch and chain, the funds for which would be raised through subscriptions. These subscriptions, it was suggested, should be limited to a maximum of 10*s* 6*d* to allow more people to donate, and everything over the £50 needed to purchase the gift would be donated to the Christmas Parcel Fund. An illuminated address would also be presented. The council's hands were tied with regards to rewarding Todger in the way they would have liked, and the suggested gift of a watch and chain fell extremely short of what was considered to be worthy. One man in attendance, by the name of Walter Millington, highlighted that the scheme 'did not seem to him to have been drawn in any sense of proportion'.[24]

Millington's opinion was reported:

> For the first time in history Runcorn had been honoured as few town's were honoured. He considered that Private Joneses deed surpassed any other deed in the whole history of the war. To offer a gold watch and chain in recognition of such services seemed to him to be a paltry thing. If Runcorn could not raise far and away beyond that Runcorn would be shamed for everlasting.[25]

Millington highlighted that there were at least 6,000 working men in Runcorn, 'and a subscription of a shilling each would bring £300':

> The sum it was suggested should be spent was less than would be realised by a penny subscription from every one. The working men of Runcorn were ready

> and willing to subscribe. A gold watch and chain was all very well in its way, but there were at least two other bodies of people in the town with whom Jones was associated that intended to do something on their own accounts, and neither could offer him less than a gold watch and chain. He suggested that £220 should be the amount aimed at, and, in addition to the gold watch and chain, the titles deeds of the house in which Private Jones's parents live should be purchased and presented through him to them with the idea that the gift should eventually revert to him.[26]

Millington reasserted his opinion that the suggested recognition was not enough. His idea of purchasing the house of his parents was a somewhat creative attempt at an indirect financial reward for Todger, who resided with his parents and who would inherit the house. As such, the council dismissed it as contravening the army order that had been set out.

Mr Dudley chipped in, saying that he felt sure Todger would wish for some recognition for his parents, who he described as belonging 'to an old Runcorn stock, and [who] were the type who had made this town'.[27] Dudley thought 'the generosity of the people of the town should be tested, and that if money came freely a proportion might be contributed', then so be it; any leftover funds could be gifted to the Christmas Fund.[28]

However, 'Mr. Imison urged that the matter should be looked at from a broad standpoint':

> There would be many Victoria Cross men up and down the country, and it would be unfortunate if some only got £20, while others got big sums. It would be a great pity if any sort of soreness was created amongst those who had earned this honour on account of different treatment. It might be the effect of that sort of thing that had caused the Government to limit gifts to soldiers. It was possible that they might have others attaining honour of the same description, and the question arose as to whether they were prepared to treat all in the same way. He did not think that the recipient would measure the town's appreciation by figures on a piece of paper.[29]

A fund was duly established.

At the council meeting, further suggestions had been put forward. Maj. Timmins, the CO of the Runcorn Volunteers, raised the idea of a tablet being installed in the drill hall. This idea would not happen straight away, but later, in 1918, it did come to fruition.

The morning after coming home, Todger visited his old school. The headmaster, Mr. Lindsay, who had taught Todger many years earlier, introduced him to the pupils who were said to be simply in awe of him. Todger then presented a number of certificates and Vere Foster prizes, which were awarded annually to students for their handwriting, on behalf of the school. He also provided a few words where he 'spoke to the boys of the points of character evidenced in his noble deed.... After the presentation of prizes, Mr Smith, who taught in this school during the time that Tom Jones was in attendance, gave him a solid silver cigarette case...'[30]

The case was engraved: 'Pte. Thomas Jones, V.C. Old Boy Runcorn Parish School Boy's School from the Staff'. It would be the first of many gifts that Todger would receive during his stint at home. Todger's visit, the first of two that he would make during his leave, caused a great deal of excitement among those at the school, particularly the pupils, who were delighted to be informed that a special school holiday was to be introduced in Todger's honour. The visit to his old school ended with the boys singing a series of patriotic songs, with 'Auld Lang Syne' wrapping things up.

Accompanied by his brothers and a press photographer, Todger then travelled to the salt works where he had been employed as a fitter before the war. His arrival met with the same giddy response, and it was clear from the reaction of the ladies that being a 'VC war hero' held much appeal to the opposite sex. His work friends presented him with a silver teapot.

In summing up his day's endeavours, one newspaper stated:

> 'Todger' Jones spent a comparatively quiet day in his native town of Runcorn of Friday. In the morning he visited his old school, was received by Headmaster Lindsay, his former teacher, and had a great ovation from the boys.
>
> In the afternoon he went to the works of the Salt Union, where he was formerly employed, and was 'lionised' by the girl emploes [*sic.*], who crowded to shake hands with him.[31]

The next day (Saturday), Todger attended a local football match between Runcorn and the Salt Union, where he kicked off the game as the guest of honour.

Later that day, he received a visit from a *Chester Chronicle* reporter, who interviewed him. Yet again, Todger gave an account of what he had done to get his VC. Notably, he paid particular attention to the bravery of his friend, Sam Poxon, who he considered 'The Bravest Man in the British Army':

> In the cosy front room of his home in Princess-street, Private Jones related to a 'Chronicle' representative the story of how he won the V.C.
>
> 'The incident happened on September 25th,' he began. 'Our orders were to take the village of [Morval]. We took it, and got through to the edge of the wood outside. We were next ordered to dig ourselves in, and consolidate the position. After working for a minute or two bullets started coming all round. I turned to the officer and said, 'If we don't get without those chaps over there, sir, they're going to make it warm for us.' He replied, 'We can't go over there, you get on with your digging.' I said, 'Alright, sir,' and began working. The bullets started coming again.

Some chaps were standing behind, and one of them got hit in the leg. Looking in the direction of the Germans, I saw what looked like the white flag.

'I'll Die Fighting'

I said to the officer, 'Do you see that, sir?' 'What do you think about them. Come on, let's go and have it out with them.' The officer said 'No'. I said, 'If I've got to be killed, I'll die fighting, not digging.' With that I jumped up, and went towards the Germans. On the way a bullet went through my steel helmet, and four bullets went through my tunic. I got across safely, and made for the end of the German trench, into which I jumped. By getting in at the end only one man at a time could hurt me. There were three Germans in the 'bay.' I happened to get without the three. Other chaps came up, but I still had only one at a time to deal with. I had the whole magazine going, and kept getting them as they came. Others rushed into their dugouts, and shouted at me. At length, I was by myself. They had all gone into their dugouts.

Germans Killed with German Bombs

I got hold of some of their bombs, undid the tape, and flung them down a dugout. The result was that three chaps came up shouting 'comrade'. I had my rifle ready. I asked, 'What's it going to be? Do you want taking prisoners? Can any of you speak English?' One man replied that he could speak good English, and in answer to a question, said that there were about 15 more Germans about. I said, 'Go and tell them they can either be taken prisoner or killed. My mates are coming across in thousands, and if they find anything wrong with me they'll cut you to bits.' He went down and told them this. 'What do they say?' I asked him when he came back. 'They're quite willing to go as prisoners,' he said. I said, 'Tell them that anyone who comes up with arms or equipment will get shot straight away.' The German position was a great natural hollow. They came out of their dugout and lined up. I can tell you I felt a bit funny. I thought 'How am I going to get this lot?' I said to myself, 'What hope they have got!' I stared at them wondering what to do, and relying upon someone coming.

Private Jones' Presence of Mind

I knew that British Troops wold come sooner or later. To kill time I said, 'Where you're going to-night it will be very cold. You will want your great coats.' The chap who could speak English said, 'Have we permission to get them?' I said, 'Yes, two at a time.' In eight or nine minutes all the Germans had got their coats. One bloke—'I didn't like the look of him'—said, 'Have I permission.' Of course I told him he had, but kept half an eye on him. When he got to the dugout about

50 yards away he made a dash for it. I swung round, click went my rifle, and he was shot through—you know. I asked if anyone else wanted to escape. They all jumped up and threw their arms up. I laughed like blazes at this. I couldn't help it. It did me good.

Welcome Assistance

I happened just then to look in the direction I had come from, and saw that some of our chaps had started from our lines. There were Poxon a Stoke man; Lance-Corporal Critchlow, a Sergeant-major, and another chap; I don't know who he was. Poxon is a stretcher-bearer, and a very brave fellow. He helped to round the Germans up. There were 130 of them, including a German General Staff Officer. Poxon is a good chum. A better man you couldn't wish for. He has gone out, not once, but hundreds of times, and it's marvellous how he pulled through. He had gone over with us when we have been on bombing attacks. He has carried the wounded for miles. He deserves an award, and it's a shame he hasn't got it.

A Big Yell

It seems that when Poxon was told where I was, he said 'If Todger's over there, I'll fetch him whether he's dead or alive.' My heart went up when I saw Poxon coming. It were grand to see him! He first gave me a clout on the ear. That was his way of greeting me. I said, 'What do you think of this lot, Sammy?' He said 'There's some souvenirs down there.' There were British regiments on my right and left, and the officers saw what happened through their field glasses.'

It was on the 26th October that Jones got to know of the King's intention to confer the V.C. upon him. 'As he was going to the post transport,' he continued, 'a man asked me if my name was Jones. I told him it was. Then he asked me if I had a Victoria Cross. I said, 'No, but I've got an Iron Cross if you've got any money to buy it.' He replied, No, I don't mean that; it's right. I wanted to know if he was 'potty', and told him to go away. He hopped it. Then the sergeant came up and offered his hand and said, 'Put it there.' I said 'What the ---- [censored in original newspaper article] up with you all this morning?' He said 'It's all right, I'm glad to shake hands with you.'

A Chap from Northwich

Then the transport sergeant came over. He's a chap from Northwich, Sergeant Smith. 'Put it there, and the best of luck to you,' he says. I said, 'Look here sergeant, will you tell me what's the matter with you all.' He gave me a telegram from the depot at Chester: 'Heartiest congratulations from all ranks at the depot,

> Cooper.' I thought, 'What's up.' Then I got a notification from headquarters, and realised what it was.
>
> The Men Still There
>
> Private Jones went on to say that he would like to make an appeal on behalf of the men who had spent two winters in the trenches. He was strongly of opinion that these brave fellows ought to be relieved, and to be allowed considerable time away from the fighting. He did not make the appeal on behalf of soldiers who had spent most of their time in billets, but those who had been fighting almost continuously since the outbreak of war.
>
> Private Jones was quite willing to give praise to the enemy where it was due. A number of Germans he described as brave fellows, who died with their hands at their guns.[32]

The day after his interview (Sunday 12th), Todger attended a parade held in his honour by the St Paul's Wesleyan Church. Alongside Maj. Timmins and the Highfield Band, Todger headed the procession. The parade left the drill hall on Greenway Road and marched down through the town. Various home defence units, together with the Runcorn detachment of the Cheshire Regiment, soldiers who were home on leave, and an assortment of others, formed the procession, with the crowds once again lining the streets.

Over the next few days, Todger visited a multitude of places. Almost all of them resulted in him being presented him with some form of gift in honour of his deed. These included a gold watch and chain, a silver engraved wristwatch, a smoker's cabinet, and some field glasses. Many more gifts would come later.

Thursday evening was spent at the local Waterloo Hotel where Todger dined with his old comrades of the Runcorn Volunteers. The following morning, he departed by train for London, where he was to receive his VC from King George V at Buckingham Palace.

8

The Closest of Friends

It is well-documented that Todger, during his interviews, was constantly talking of others whose deeds did not get any recognition. He had great respect for his fellow soldiers and was quick to lavish praise on them, particularly those who had been at the front since the start.

However, of all the men Todger served with, there was one who stood out—someone who he had the greatest of respect for. Todger called him 'The Bravest Man in the British Army.'[1] That man was Sam Poxon.

Time and time again, Todger made a point of highlighting Poxon's reckless bravery and he went out of his way to ensure people knew what type of a man Poxon was. Therefore, in keeping with Todger's wish to have his friend's efforts recognised, it is very fitting to delve deeper into Poggy's life and to single him out here for special mention.

Prior to the war, Sam Poxon was employed as a miner. He hailed from Stoke and enlisted in Longton, Staffordshire, in November 1914, at the age of thirty-three. He held the rank of private and was posted to the 1st Cheshires.

Poxon's records show that he was a widow and in a relationship with Sarah Anne Podmore at the time of his enlistment. They had lived together for ten years and had five children between them. They were married the following year, on 9 November 1915, at Stoke Registry Office.

It is not clear exactly when Todger and Poggy became best pals, but it is possible that their bond was forged, or began to flourish, in England in 1914, prior to them going to the front. They trained together at Birkenhead and Codford, so at the very least they would have been acquainted with one and other at this point.

Poggy's transition from miner to an actively serving soldier was extremely swift. Despite not having any previous military experience, he would receive a mere seventy days' training before being shipped off to serve with the battalion at the front where he served as a stretcher-bearer. Todger and Poxon sailed in the same batch of reinforcements, arriving in France in the third week of January 1915.[2]

Todger and Poxon's friendship would prove to be infallible on the battlefields of France and Flanders, and the two men greatly admired the other's qualities as a soldier. They certainly had a lot in common and were cut from the same cloth. They were of a similar age; Todger being born in 1880 and Poxon in 1881. They were older than many of their comrades and this may have contributed to their friendship, but there were other similarities too. Both were very plucky individuals, but like many a brave man, they had the occasional issue with authority and were prone to the odd lapse of discipline. In short, both men had a habit of getting into mischief.

Both men also went 'missing' at some point in the war. In Poggy's case, he had succeeded very early in his military career in stirring the water when, on Christmas Eve 1914, with just a few weeks' service under his belt, he went missing from camp. The date, incidentally, also coincided with Todger's birthday, which was Christmas Day.

Poxon returned to camp with his tail between his legs four days later. He received a surprisingly mild punishment in the form of the forfeiture of six days' pay. Not one to be beaten, Todger pulled the same stunt the following year during the Christmas period of 1915, although by that time, they were on active service and his punishment was more severe.

Just one month after arriving in France, Poxon was reprimanded once again, this time for leaving a trench without permission, for which he was docked seven days' pay. There could have been several reasons for Poxon committing his 'crime', but, unfortunately, details are not forthcoming.

An interesting possibility is that he left the trench under good intentions. In his book, *There's a Devil in the Drum*, John Lucy, an Irishman who was commissioned from the ranks of the Royal Irish Rifles, recounted an incident where a man had ran out to a wounded comrade against orders. Another man had already attempted it and died trying, and others had been forbidden due to the risk. According to Lucy, the man went out anyway and was successful in his rescue mission. Not only that, but he also carried in his dead comrade who had been killed while attempting the same feat. Nevertheless, the man 'was casually tried and punished for disobeying trench standing orders'.[3]

Whether or not Poxon's act of leaving the trench was for the recovery of a wounded man against orders will never be known, but all things considered, it is perhaps unlikely. On the day in question, the battalion was in divisional reserve.[4] Furthermore, the battalion war diary has no entry other than to say where they were, hinting perhaps that nothing worthy of note took place and that no casualties were sustained, although this does not cancel out the possibility of men from other nearby units being wounded.[5]

Todger could quite easily have met with a similar punishment for his own act of indiscipline at Morval on 25 September 1916, when he disobeyed a direct order not to leave his trench, but since he returned with over 100 prisoners, his act of disobedience can perhaps be forgiven on that occasion.

Despite their similarities, the roles of the two men were tremendously contrasted in nature. Todger became a bomber and marksman and Poxon became a battalion stretcher-bearer—a role that did not require him to be armed. While Todger tried his best to end lives with his bombs and bayonet, Poxon was alongside him, trying his best to patch up and save the lives of those who fell. Todger and Poxon may have fulfilled very different roles during their time at the front, but both were typical examples of the stalwart Tommy Atkins at his finest.

Battalion stretcher-bearers are popularly known as the unsung heroes of the war, and a great many were decorated for their selfless bravery. The most notable is William Coltman of the North Staffs who, in addition to the VC, was awarded a DCM and bar (two DCMs), and a MM and bar (two MMs). Coltman, who survived the war, became the most decorated 'other rank' in the British Army.

Battalion stretcher-bearers were the first response to battlefield casualties. Unlike RAMC stretcher-bearers who relayed the wounded behind the lines, the battalion bearers were required to enter no-man's-land to retrieve casualties, often under heavy fire. They provided only basic medical assistance in the form of stemming blood loss and keeping the wounded man alive long enough to be treated more thoroughly by a medical officer. After they had patched up casualties, the battalion bearers would either carry them from the field or leave them in a shell hole or another form of relative cover from where they could be picked up later, depending on circumstances. Battalion stretcher-bearers were trained infantrymen, but they did not carry weapons.

Battalion stretcher-bearers generally numbered four to a company (sixteen per battalion). They came under the charge of the battalion medical officer who belonged to the RAMC but was attached to a specific infantry battalion. Noel Chavasse, the recipient of the VC and bar, for example, was attached to the Liverpool Scottish and served with them both prior to and during the war.

From his aid post, the medical officer would treat those men that his bearers brought in. These bearers were not required to venture any further back than this. It was the job of the RAMC men to take the casualties further down the line and through to the next staging posts.

Sam Poxon was well known for his contempt of danger and complete disregard for his own safety when endeavouring to help the wounded, and Todger said that his friend had carried wounded comrades for miles. His methods in tending to those who had been hit, although somewhat unorthodox, added greatly to his reputation.

Stretcher-bearers were not expected to go over the top with the battalion. If a wave of men was set to attack, the bearers would follow up behind them to assist those who had fallen in the charge. They did not, as a rule, accompany the men in the initial attack. Poxon, however, utterly disregarded this notion. He wanted to be 'on the spot' the second a man fell so he could offer assistance in the shortest possible time. Instead of following his comrades, Poxon simply accompanied them by taking part in the attack with them. If this meant him taking part in charges completely unarmed, then so be it, that is what he would do.

When Todger was home on leave following the award of his VC, he made the point of mentioning Poxon's bravery to those he spoke to.

In one interview, he related:

> I have seen—acts by the score—acts that deserve the honour that was given to those who performed them. There are no words to describe the grandeur of courage of some men in the face of the relentless enemy and I am proud to think that the bravest man in the British Army today is a pal of mine.
>
> His name is Sam Poxon and he's a stretcher-bearer with the Cheshires, but he's got no medal to show what he's done. He's got nothing but a healed up wound. He's a Stoke lad, is Poggy, and has the biggest heart that ever beat under khaki. He's been out there right from the start—and many a dozen have showered blessings on him. He's one of the sort that doesn't know what fear is, after the Cheshires have gone, he's gone—not after them, always with them. He's always in the thick of it is Poggy and never carries no weapons. All he's armed with is a roll of bandage and a bottle of iodine. The fighting doesn't interest him all that much but he keeps his eyes peeled. He's always on the watch, and when some poor beggar gets it and screams in agony, the man on the spot quick is Poxon.[6]

As can be seen in his interview with the reporter, Todger was somewhat frustrated that Poxon had not been decorated for the many deeds of bravery he had performed. Todger was particularly angry that Poxon had not been recognised for his gallantry at Falfemont Farm in early September 1916, where he had gone into the attack alongside the men and worked tirelessly to treat and rescue them under heavy fire. Todger had played a prominent part in the same attack and had been one of the first to enter the German trenches, which he then bombed, gaining a souvenir in the form of the Iron Cross in the process, but despite his own stellar performance, Todger was of the opinion that it was Poxon who had excelled himself that day.

It seems that Todger, at the time of his interview, was unaware that Poxon had in fact been recommended for the MM, 'For Bravery in the Field', for the Falfemont Farm action and that this award was duly granted to Poxon. It was confirmed in *The London Gazette* in November that year while Todger was at home on leave.[7]

The fact that Todger was on leave may explain why he seems to not have known about Poxon's award. That said, it is somewhat perplexing that, even in 1925, when speaking of his friend, Todger still seemed to be in the dark about Poxon's medal.[8] Perhaps Poxon did not think to mention it to Todger after the latter's return to the battalion from England in 1917. Poxon was certainly a modest individual, as noted by Todger, who, when referring to his friend's bravery, explained that he was not the sort to say what he had done.

In further words of praise, Todger would say:

> There must be very few men who have been under fire so often and so long as he's been, and lived to tell of it....
>
> It's a mistake to think all the heroes belong to those who got Huns. Every stretcher-bearer takes his life in his hands every day. It's hard, risky work, they're a grand lot—and Poxon is the grandest of them. I know his idea of what duty is—I've seen what he does—and I tell you straight, the bravest man I ever met is Sam Poxon of the Cheshire Regiment.[9]

Poxon was the first man to dash out to support Todger during his VC act at Morval. He had not witnessed Todger leaving their trench and was unaware of what had happened until he had asked others for Todger's whereabouts. As soon as he heard of what Todger had done, he did not hesitate in going over after him. Todger's act that resulted in his VC may have turned out very differently had Poxon not reacted the way he did. Only after Poxon had jumped up to go across did others get up and do the same. Had Poxon not been there, it is distinctly possible that the others would not have gone off their own back and the chances are Todger would have remained unsupported in something of a fix with his prisoners. Simply put, Poxon had set an example, and his actions had inspired others to follow him. This ensured Todger made it back with his prisoners and his life.

When describing the moment Poxon arrived at the German trench, Todger said Poxon greeted him with the words: 'Hello Todger, what the ---- [censored in original article] are you doing?' He then started laughing and slapped Todger across the earhole.[10]

When asked if 'the lads raised a yell' as the prisoners were brought back, Todger was quick to change the subject, replying: 'Yell? You should have heard it!' 'And here,' recorded Todger's interviewer, 'Private Jones broke off to speak in the highest possible praise of Poxon':

> That chap has deserved more recognition hundreds of times. He is a stretcher-bearer, and goes out after wounded many and many a time, and has carried scores of wounded lads in. He risks his life over and over again to save other lads. He deserves something. It is a shame he has not had it before now. He's as brave a fellow as there is in the army. When he knew I had gone across he said, 'I'm going after Todger wherever he is, and I'll bring him back alive or dead.' I tell you it was grand to see him.[11]

In another account, Todger described seeing someone start from the British lines. Initially he did not know who it was, but he soon realised:

> It was my chum [Poxon] coming to look for me. He had been asking where I was and when they told him, he said: 'If Todger's across there, I'm going to fetch him, dead or alive!' They all thought I was a 'goner,' but, when they saw my chum start, three more chaps—a sergeant-major, a corporal and stretcher bearer, came across with him. Seeing I was alive, my chum gave me a smack on the face and couldn't stop larking.[12]

The two men had a mutually keen interest in souvenirs. Todger certainly had a fondness for such items, and souvenirs had been the first thing on Poxon's mind when he saw Todger's prisoners.

On 4 April 1917, Poxon sustained serious gunshot wounds to his foot from either small arms fire or shrapnel, but more than likely the latter. Unbeknown to him at the time, Poxon's wound brought his active service with the Cheshire Regiment to an end.

Three days after receiving his wound, Poxon was evacuated to England where he would spend the next few months recovering. It was not until 27 August that Poxon was able to return to the regiment's reserve battalion. He later transferred to a protection company of the Royal Defence Corps (RDC). This was a home defence unit whose main tasks were to guard POW camps, docks and munitions camps, and any other areas that were deemed vulnerable to German infiltration.[13]

Poxon's service with the RDC was relatively brief, but within that short space of time, he displayed various degrees of disobedience and distain for authority; more than once, his wayward behaviour landed him in trouble. As a consequence, he suffered some loss of pay and was confined to barracks, though some of his offences were not as severe as others.

On 17 September 1917, he was found not to have shaved when on company inspection—a crime that cost him two days' confined to barracks (CB). On 19 April, the following year, while at Wexford, he received two days' CB for 'creating a noise in barracks' before 'going absent after lights out'.[14]

Company Sgt-Maj. Murray is recorded as a witness to Poxon's above antics. Murray, together with Acting-Sergeants Cooke and Taylor, was also witness to Poxon's behaviour on 2 May 1918 when he refused 'to leave the canteen at 9.30 p.m. when requested by the NCO in charge'.[9] This refusal to obey orders landed Poxon with the loss of seven days' pay and seven days' confined to barracks.

In July 1918, Poxon was discharged to the Army Reserve (Class 'P') and returned to work in the mines.[15] Owing to an 'accident' attributed to his war service, he was listed as having a 20-per cent disability and issued with a Silver War Badge.

Poxon moved around different addresses in Stoke in the years following the Armistice, and during the Second World War, just before his retirement, he worked at an ammunitions factory at Radway Green. He passed away in his mid-seventies.

In all likelihood, despite their close friendship, Todger and Poxon probably did not see each other again after Poxon was evacuated from the front after being wounded. Todger returned to Runcorn and Poggy to Stoke-on-Trent, but neither man ever forgot the other.

Samuel Poxon's grandson, Spencer Browning, remembers his grandfather speaking of Todger: 'More than once he would turn to my grandmother and say, "Sal, I wonder what Todger is doing now."'[16]

Spencer, who was sixteen years old when his grandfather died, also recalls an impressive illuminated address on the wall at his grandfather's house. He remembers it as 'a beautiful thing'. An article from the *Stoke Sentinel* suggests that Todger had something to do with its creation:

> While Todger was fairly ambivalent about his own award, he was outraged that Poggy had been denied a medal. He was instrumental in commissioning an 'illuminated address', a commemorative plaque in recognition of Poggy's bravery, which was paid for by the men and officers of the battalion.[17]

'It was 2ft by 18ins,' recalls Poxon's grandson, 'and it said he was in the thick of it and should have had a medal.'[18]

According to the article, Spencer Browning thought: 'Mr Jones was not only a man of rare courage, but a man of equally rare humility and loyalty'. In summing up the fact that Todger thought Poxon 'the bravest man in the British Army', Spencer succulently noted: 'From a man of his stature, it was praise indeed, worth more than any medal'.[19]

Once again, however, we are left with the impression that Todger remained unaware of Poxon's MM, and the *Stoke Sentinel* article also leans towards this belief. Not only that, but the wording of the article also suggests that Poxon's family were not aware of his award. It is indeed a mystery and very intriguing to think that his closest friend, and his own family, may never have been aware that he had been decorated for his bravery in the war. If this is the case, it is hoped that this chapter will reach the family of Sam 'Poggy' Poxon, 'the bravest man in the British Army', so they can learn that his bravery was recognised after all.

A Note on Poxon's Name

The various newspaper articles quoted in this chapter differ in their spelling of 'Poxon'. Incorrect variants include 'Pogson' and 'Bogson'. These have been corrected/edited here to avoid confusion and to provide some uniformity to the text. The mistakes have occurred, no doubt, when Todger was verbally describing the events to the reporters, who misunderstood what he had said.

It was for this reason that the identity of Poxon had eluded for me many years.

9

'How the Dickens did you do it Jones'?

After returning home from the front, Todger travelled to London where he was to be presented with his VC at the hand of the king at Buckingham Palace. The ceremony took place on 18 November and involved around 200 soldiers who were to be decorated with a variety of medals for their wide-ranging deeds of bravery. Many of these awards were for actions during the Battle of the Somme, which, by coincidence, ended on the day of the ceremony.

In addition to Todger, four other men received the VC that day. These were 2Lt Gabriel George Coury (South Lancashire Regiment), Sgt George Sanders (West Yorkshire Regiment); Pte Albert Hill (Royal Welsh Fusiliers), and Pte William Jackson (17th Australian Imperial Force (AIF)).[1]

A number of other notable men were present, including flying ace Capt. Albert Ball, who received the DSO with two bars and a MC in the ceremony. Ball would later receive a posthumous VC, and at the time of his death, he was Britain's leading flying ace with forty-four victories to his name.

Capt. Edward Unwin of the Royal Navy was awarded the CMG at the ceremony. He was already the recipient of the VC, having been awarded it in January 1916 for actions in April 1915 at Gallipoli.

As his turn came, Todger's name was read out: '11000 Pte. Thomas Alfred Jones, Cheshire Regiment'. This was his cue. Todger nervously approached the king as the official citation was read out:

> For most conspicuous bravery. He was with his company consolidating the defences in front of a village, and, noticing an enemy sniper at 200 yards distance, he went out, and, though one bullet went through his coat, he returned the sniper's fire and killed him. He then saw two more of the enemy firing at him, although displaying a white flag. Both of these he also shot. On reaching the enemy trench he found several occupied dug-outs, and single-handed,

Contemporary illustrations show Todger threatening his captives who are in a state of fear with grenades.

A triumphant and somewhat relaxed Todger Jones stands above his prisoners who hold their hands high in surrender.

A cigarette card depicting Pte Thomas Alfred 'Todger' Jones issued by Gallaher Ltd as part of a series in 1917. (*Victoria Cross Heroes 7th Series of 25*)

Todger stands over his newly captured prisoners who stand in the 'hollow' with their hands up. Meanwhile, the redoubtable Sam Poxon dashes forward to support his best friend. (*Artist: Steve Noon, author's collection*)

The author (Neil Thornton) provides members of the Mercian Regiment with a narrative of Todger's bravery at his statue, following the regiment's freedom of the borough march in December 2014. (*Martin Kilduff*)

Left: Todger's steel helmet is displayed in the Cheshire Regiment military museum in Chester. The bullet hole was inflicted by a German sniper on 25 September 1916 as Todger launched his one-man attack. (*Mark Green, Victoria Cross Online*)

Below: Todger's war medals were donated to the regimental museum by his sister, Emily. The group takes pride of place in the museum's extensive collection. (*Mark Green, Victoria Cross Online*)

This detailed mural is situated a mere stone's throw to where Princess Street was situated and where Todger 'bolted' to avoid the crowds during his VC homecoming. The mural features various local subjects of note, including Todger Jones. (*Mural artists Fiona and Neil Osborne from One Red Shoe*)

Todger's territorial medal (right), seen here with his twenty-five years' workplace service medal. These were not donated to the museum with his Great War medals. Together with various other items, they remain with the family. (*Percy Dunbavand*)

Above: Todger is buried in Runcorn Cemetery. From this angle, Victoria Road School is visible. During Todger's funeral, the schoolchildren watched proceedings from the upper windows.

Below: Todger is hurled into the air by a shell explosion. As a result, he was nursing a painful shoulder wound at the time of his VC act that occurred later that month. (*Artist: Eric Thornton*)

Right: Todger chats with wounded servicemen following his return to Runcorn in November 1916. They had rushed down from the hospital to greet him on his return.

Below: A press photograph showing soldiers advancing towards Morval on 25 September 1916.

Todger's government-issue paving stone is located directly in front of his statue. It was unveiled on the centenary of his VC act by Percy Dunbavand (Todger's great nephew) and the mayor of Halton. Standard-bearers from the Regimental Association stand either side of the statue while the lord lieutenant of Cheshire and Neil Thornton (author) observe proceedings from the right.

Todger prepares to throw a German grenade into a dugout during his VC act. (*Artist: Eric Thornton*)

RUNCORN V.C.
SERVES AGAIN

Right: A newspaper cutting from the Second World War reporting that Todger is now in uniform again, serving with the Home Guard.

Below left: Todger's Liberal Club medallion was presented to him after the war in a ceremony where each of the club's members received one. A number of posthumous medallions were presented to the next-of-kin of those who had lost their lives, including Todger's brother, Arthur. (*Paul Smitham*)

Below right: The reverse of Todger's Liberal Club medallion, with his details engraved. (*Paul Smitham*)

Above: Local children play in the shattered remnants of St Eloi. It was here where Todger took part in one of his first battles in 1915.

Below: Todger rallies those around him who are without orders before leading them forward during the act for which he was awarded the DCM. Todger showed an incredible degree of leadership and situation awareness during the battle. (*Artist: Eric Thornton*)

Thomas William Jones Abram, Todger's son, seen here in 1941 with his wife, Minnie, and daughter, Edna. (*Percy Dunbavand*)

A German sniper takes aim. Todger was fired at by more than one enemy marksman while crossing no-man's-land at Morval. (*Artist: Eric Thornton*)

Above: Todger shakes hands with King George V during the royal visit to his hometown in 1925. Standing to Todger's left (nearest the camera wearing his campaign medal) is Thomas Taylor. Thomas Moffatt stands to Todger's right. Both of these men defended the Rorke's Drift mission station during the Zulu War.

Left: Todger's brother, Arthur, who was shot in the head by a sniper on what was his first day in the frontline. He underwent four operations and had a metal plate fitting to his skull before passing away in 1917. (*Percy Dunbavand*)

A close-up of the silver cigarette case presented to Todger 'as a small token in recognition of his gallant conduct', on behalf of the warrant officers and sergeants of the regiment at Bidston Camp. (*David Copland*)

The shattered remnants of Morval after it was captured. This *Daily Mail* postcard is captioned: 'The last state of Morval, captured 25th September 1916'.

RUNCORN V.C. ROUNDING UP HIS PRISONERS.

The above is the official photo of Private T. Jones at the head of the 100 Germans whom he captured and disarmed single-handed, marching them back to the British lines. In a vivid account of how Private Jones accomplished this amazing performance, an eye-witness writes:—

When his chums came across they said it was the finest sight they had ever seen. I tell you there was a shout went up. There was "Todger" standing by 100 Germans in a hollow. He was ordering them to put on their coats. With his pals he rounded them up and brought them back, including a General Staff officer.

An original newspaper clipping of the widely-circulated photo purporting to depict Todger marching his prisoners to the rear. He was presented with a framed version of the photograph by Mrs Roscoe Brunner.

Devonshire Square, 'the principal thoroughfare', seen here in 1907, where Todger fought his way through the crowds before running home down a side street.

THE LEEDS MERCURY. MONDAY. NOVEMBER 20, 1916.

THE LEEDS V.C. RECEIVES HIS DECORATION FROM THE KING.

Above: The four VCs. Photograph taken as they left the palace following the presentation of their medals. *From left to right*: Sgt Davis, Pte 'Todger' Jones, Sgt Sanders, and Pte Hill.

Right: Todger shows his parents the bullet hole in his steel helmet after arriving home from the front. One wonders whether they wanted to laugh or cry at their son's near-death experience.

DAILY NEWS AND LEADER, MOND

V.C.'s TROPHY OF THE BATTLEFIELD.

Private "Todger" Jones, the Runcorn V.C., who captured 102 German prisoners single-handed, showing his parents a bullet hole in his steel helmet.

Above: Todger (second right, front row) dressed in his 'hospital blues' as a patient in the Vicarage Hospital. His father stands behind him with his hand raised to his chest.

Left: Todger smiles for the camera at the back of his home in Princess Street in November 1916.

Todger (right) posing in later life with Hugh Covlin who was awarded his VC for actions in 1917 with the 9th Battalion. They are the only two men in the Cheshire Regiment to be awarded the VC.

The procession for Todger's funeral waits outside his home on Princess Street before setting off on their journey. The funeral was a large occasion with many dignitaries and military figures present. (*Percy Dunbavand*)

VICTORIA CROSS CENTENARY CELEBRATION

(1856 — 1956)

MECCA LTD

present a

TEA PARTY AND CABARET

Thursday, 28th June, 1956
3.30 p.m to 5.30 p.m.

LYCEUM — THE STRAND

SOUVENIR PROGRAMME

Todger passed away in January 1956. In June that year, one of his nephew's attended the VC 'Tea Party and Cabaret', which was held in recognition of the centenary of the award. As can be seen, Todger's nephew obtained several signatures to his programme. (*Percy Dunbavand*)

An illustration from the *World Wide* magazine, *c.* 1917. Todger stands over the Prussian Guard officer he defeated in hand-to-hand combat. Todger then acquired his slain enemy's Iron Cross as a souvenir.

Above left: Leonard Pollit was the first man of the 5th Chesires to receive the DCM. Pollit travelled home to Runcorn from London with Todger in November 1916. (*Gary Bentley*).

Above right: Arthur Greg, seen here some time after being wounded after leading a bombing attack at Hill 60 in 1915. A large scar across the lower side of Greg's face is clearly visible. Greg was later killed with the RFC. Todger was one of only a handful to survive the action unscathed.

Todger Jones

Left: A somewhat grainy image of Todger in the latter stage of life.

Below: The Vicarage served as an auxiliary hospital during the war, treating those who were suffering from light wounds and illness. Reverend Perrin (later Canon Perrin) stands second from right. He was the honorary chaplain, and was awarded the OBE for his services during the war. (*Peter Blackmore, Vice-Chairman of The Runcorn & District Historical Society*)

"IF YOU ONLY KNEW." FOR MADGE AMBROSE'S CHARMING NEW SERIAL STORY FIRST LONG INSTALMENT TO-MORROW.

DAILY SKETCH

Friday 10 NOVEMBER

GREAT HOME WELCOME TO V.C. WHO TOOK 102 GERMAN PRISONERS.

Photographs published by the *Daily Sketch* capture the jubilation on the streets of Runcorn following Todger's 'Great Home Welcome'.

Todger stands near his home among friends, family, and the gathered crowd after his homecoming. His sister, Emily, is to his left.

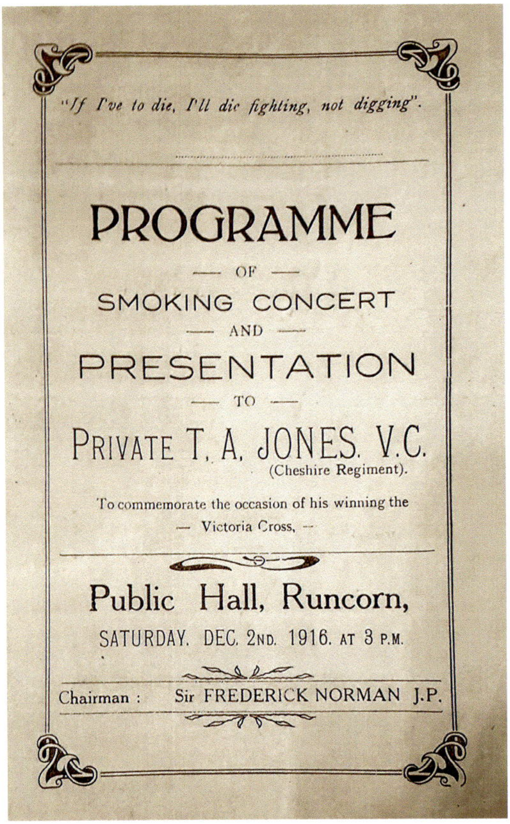

"If I've to die, I'll die fighting, not digging".

PROGRAMME
— OF —
SMOKING CONCERT
— AND —
PRESENTATION
— TO —
PRIVATE T. A. JONES. V.C.
(Cheshire Regiment).

To commemorate the occasion of his winning the
— Victoria Cross, —

Public Hall, Runcorn,
SATURDAY. DEC. 2ND. 1916. AT 3 P.M.

Chairman : Sir FREDERICK NORMAN J.P.

left: A 'smoking concert' held on 2 December saw Todger presented with various gifts, including a lifelong membership of the Liberal Club. His 4 p.m. hospital curfew meant he could only stay for an hour of his own function.

Below left: In the Second World War, after a failed attempt to enlist in the infantry on account of his age, Todger had to settle for service in the Home Guard. He patrolled the streets of Runcorn and checked identifications.

Below right: Once in the enemy trench, Todger shot down three enemy soldiers. He advanced and took out several more before bombing their dugouts. (*Artist: Eric Thornton*)

V.C.'s home comes under the axe

DEMOLITION men last week finished off the former home in Princess Street of Runcorn's greatest war hero — Thomas Alfred "Todger" Jones, who won the Victoria Cross in the Great War.

The Jones family had lived there for many years, and "Todger" himself stayed at No. 51 until his death in 1956 at the age of 76.

It was on September 26th, 1916, that "Todger," serving with the 1st Battalion The Cheshire Regiment at Morval, France, won his V.C.

During a lull in fighting after his Regiment had taken its objectives for the day, "Todger" went off towards the enemy lines looking for more action. A German sniper put a bullet through his helmet and his greatcoat for his curiosity, but "Todger," a fine shot, returned the fire and killed the sharp-shooter.

Pressing on, he came under fire from two more snipers and killed them also before passing right through the German lines to some reserve trenches.

Hearing some German voices coming from an underground dugout, "Todger" called on the occupants to surrender, which they did, twenty men giving themselves up. He repeated this performance six times along the enemy trenches and then marched 102 prisoners back through their own lines and through a British barrage to the safety of his own trenches.

His citation read that he had received the Victoria Cross for "most conspicuous bravery when his company was consolidating defences," and after his death his sister, Mrs. E. Lightfoot, presented the medal to the Regimental Museum at Chester Castle.

"Todger" Jones

"Todger" Jones's name lives on in Runcorn in darts circles, where a trophy bearing his name is still competed for.

Two years after winning the V.C., "Todger" also won the D.C.M. for taking messages five times through an intensive barrage and leading stragglers back to their positions.

He is buried in Runcorn Cemetery.

Above left: In the early 1960s, as part of the town's redevelopment, Princess Street was all but demolished. Today only a small section of the street survives.

Above right: William Allaby, Todger's good friend and work colleague who died in October 1915 while serving onboard HMS *Velox*.

A view from the Runcorn war memorial, looking down Greenway Road. The memorial garden where Todger's statue is situated can be seen on the right.

Right: Pte Joseph Edward Jones, Todger's nephew. Joseph would suffer terribly as a result of the war and is said to have never been the same man afterwards. (*Anne Bamber*)

Below: A youthful Todger Jones sits on the extreme left during annual camp in Wales during his earlier years with the volunteers. (*Percy Dunbavand*)

POST CARD

Correspondence. Address

Just a line to say we are having very hot weather Still waiting for Friday Tom

Mrs Jones
39 Princess St
Runcorn
Cheshire

The reverse of the postcard from 'Tom' to his mother, 'just a line to say we are having very hot weather'. (*Percy Dunbavand*)

Todger enjoys the attention of well-wishers in Runcorn, *c*. November 1916.

The indomitable Sam Poxon, seen here at his daughter's wedding (second from right), and with his wife and first daughter (bottom image). (*Stoke Sentinel*)

Left: Todger's parents, Edward and Elizabeth Jones. The aging couple were immensely proud of their son. They regularly accompanied him to the many events and functions he attended.

Below: Todger is raised shoulder high with friends and family. His father stands to the extreme left with his hand in the air.

The Todger Jones' dart competition was named as such due to his interest and ability as a darts player. This trophy was awarded to Eric Thornton (grandfather of the author) for reaching the 1965 semi-final.

Left: In 1920, Todger attended King George V's garden party at Buckingham Palace. He can be seen sitting in the centre in the third row from the front, surrounded by VC recipients.

Below: Members of a large parade gather in Runcorn. Todger stands to the front left in front of the officers.

Above left: Studio portrait of Todger Jones taken after the award of his VC, which was later produced as a postcard. This one signed: 'With Love from Uncle Tom'. (*Anne Bamber*)

Above right: A rare pre-war photograph of Todger Jones. This image featured alongside an article on Todger upon the news that he was to be awarded the VC, prior to the plentiful amount of photographs that would later be taken.

Below: A blue plaque to Todger Jones is situated on the small surviving section of Princess Street. It is one of a series of plaques fitted around the town by local historian Stuart Allen.

Codford Camp, *c*. 1914. Todger stands on the left while those in the centre of the shot show what they intend to do to the Kaiser—i.e. cut off his head!

'If I'm going to die, I'll die fighting, not digging!' Todger mounts the parapet to launch his one-man attack. (*Artist: Eric Thornton*)

> disarmed 102 of the enemy, including three or four officers, and marched them back to our lines through a heavy barrage. He had been warned of the misuse of the white flag by the enemy, but insisted on going out after them.[2]

The king pinned the VC to Todger's chest and shook his hand before asking the question: 'How the Dickens did you do it Jones?'

'I won't tell you what I answered on the spur of the moment,' Todger later explained, 'but the King laughed. I gave him an idea of how the thing had been done, and he laughed again at the thought of me fetching home my happy little family.'[3]

After the investiture when the recipients were making their exit, Todger and the other VC men were called across to have their photo taken with Sgt George Sanders VC, who was one of the five to get it that day. A photographer local to Sanders had stopped him for a photo but, 'in characteristic modesty', he wanted his fellow VC men to be in on it and 'insisted on his comrades in honour' sharing the photographer's attention.[4] They duly took up the offer and the image was published in the *Leeds Mercury* on 20 November 1916.

Todger returned home to Runcorn, but if he was hoping for a quieter time now that his VC had been officially presented, he was to be bitterly disappointed. The modest hero's hectic and relentless schedule was set to continue in earnest.

Since his homecoming, Todger had yet to visit Chester, the home of his regiment. Now he had been presented with his VC, plans were quickly put in place. On Monday 20 November, Todger, his parents, and Sir Frederick Norman travelled to the city in style in Sir Norman's open-top car.

Sir Norman was a Cheshire magistrate and chairman of the Runcorn bench and a pioneer of applied science who was involved in the local chemical industry. His only son, Stanley, himself a promising chemist, would be killed in the closing stages of the war, which affected Sir Norman greatly.

Norman held great influence and made great efforts to help local institutions wherever he could. He was polite to all he met and he possessed a sound character, but it was said he was difficult to get to know intimately. Despite this, Sir Norman forged a solid friendship with the Joneses. He put his open-top car at their disposal and accompanied them to their engagements and provided exciting and energetic speeches to eager audiences. Sir Norman had been present at the station as Todger pulled into Runcorn after returning from the front, and he had escorted Todger's family members home through the crowds in his car, making more than one trip to ensure they all arrived safely.

En route to Chester, they stopped at the neighbouring towns of Frodsham and Helsby. They stopped at the British Insulated and Helsby Cable Works where Todger received a rousing reception. The employees who worked there were deemed to be in important work for the war effort and therefore exempt from conscription that had been introduced earlier in the year.

Todger gave the following short speech to the employees, emphasising that, although they were not fighting at the front, they were, nonetheless, doing their bit:

> I know this place, and I know that many of you must have felt sorry that you were not able to enlist. I dare say some of you have been insulted and have felt it. I know this, that your work has got to be carried out. I am an engineer, and know that somebody has got to stay behind. If you got away in the first instance you were lucky. Whatever may be your position here, we are all working towards a common end. It is organisation of the right kind that is going to win this war, and therefore I say to you the same as has been said to us, 'Carry on the good work!'[5]

At his own request, Todger and his entourage then visited the local military hospital near the works, where he chatted to the patients, two or three of whom were confined to their beds on account of their wounds.

Todger's journey through Frodsham and Helsby had deliberately been kept from the public. Both towns were disappointed at not being given the opportunity to line the streets to set eyes on the local hero and to celebrate his presence, but Todger had not wanted to endure any more fuss than was absolutely necessary.

They then made their way to the walled city of Chester, where the scenes would be reminiscent to those played out in Runcorn, only bigger. Once in the city, the remark 'There he is!' was made every few yards by spectators who recognised him from photographs that had been published. At the east gate of the city wall, they were met by the band from the Cheshire Regiment Depot, who then headed the procession to Chester Castle, playing stirring tunes as they went. Thousands of people filled the streets all the way to the Castle where members of the Cheshire Regiment were formed up on three sides of a square. Gen. Piteairn Campbell, commanding the Western Division, then arrived with his staff, the mayor of Chester, and a number of other civic dignitaries. Todger spoke with each of them and received their hearty congratulations.

Gen. Campbell gave a speech to the troops of the Cheshire Regiment, pointing out that Todger was a 'splendid fellow', highlighting that his VC was the first to the regiment. Campbell added 'that the Cheshire Regiment ought to be proud to have such a man as Private Jones, and that Cheshire had sent him into the world to do such good work for his regiment and his King and country'.[6]

Subsequently, the *Liverpool Daily Post* reported on further content from Campbell's speech:

> He was glad to say that Private Jones did well in the musketry line, for they must remember that the small British force which went out at the beginning of the war and joined the 6th [*sic.*] Division, by fine fighting and grand shooting, helped to keep back the Germans. 'Private Jones,' said the General, turning to

> the hero of the day. 'I congratulate you very much and your regiment on having such a man in it like you. I trust you will live long to wear that fine decoration you have received. I wish you good luck.'[7]

The paper also reported on Mayor Frost who was present:

> The Mayor afterwards addressed Private Jones, and said they at Chester were extremely proud of Jones, and on the city's behalf he offered him its congratulations. It was some satisfaction to him, said the Mayor, to be permitted to offer these congratulations to Private Jones, as he was one of the last men to speak to his [the mayor's] son a few minutes before his death.[8]

The article continued:

> Afterwards Colonel Neville shook hands with Jones, and the latter accompanied General Campbell and party whilst the General inspected the assembled troops. Subsequently Jones was cheered by several of his comrades, and, with the band playing stirring music, was carried triumphantly around Castle-square.
>
> Later the V.C. was entertained at dinner in the dining-hall at the Castle, his delighted parents being amongst the honoured guests.[9]

The dinner, however, was not something Todger was particularly comfortable with. He sat at the head of the hall with the dignitaries, while his comrades—who he would much sooner have been among—were sat with the guests.

Later in the evening, Todger 'escaped' out of the back door with some of his mates from the regiment and headed off into the night, thereby abandoning his own function.

On 25 November, just one week after receiving his VC, Todger was admitted to the Vicarage Hospital in Runcorn. As the name suggests, it was a vicarage that had been converted for use as a hospital for the duration of the war. It had been built in 1912 by Reverend Howard Perrin who had become the vicar of Runcorn. It replaced an older building that had fallen into a state of disrepair. On the outbreak of hostilities, Perrin, who served as an 'honorary chaplain', had eagerly offered his vicarage as an auxiliary hospital to treat men with minor wounds. Perrin would be awarded the OBE for his services during the war.

Todger's time at the hospital delayed his return to the front for a considerable time. He remained a patient for three months. The public were told he was suffering from 'septic poisoning', but his medical records state he was admitted with 'dermatitis and neurasthenia'. The latter symptom of neurasthenia is underlined, indicating perhaps that this was the main reason.

'Neurasthenia' covered a wide array of ailments, and its usage and meaning has evolved with time. During the First World War, it was often used to describe chronic fatigue and weakness brought on by psychological and mental factors, as well as physical factors. It was thought to have stemmed from exhaustion of the nervous system and was also used to describe shellshock.

Todger was admitted to hospital when he was due to return to the front, once his leave expired. It is distinctly possible that Todger was not in any fit state to return to the war. It was well-known that he was worn out upon his return to Runcorn. This had been commented on by various people and newspapers, including the *Daily Mirror*, which had reported that he was 'exhausted' after returning from the front.[10]

This would tally with the neurasthenia diagnosis. It is possible that the newspapers and general public were not informed of the true reasons behind his stay at the hospital. It was far better for a hero to be suffering from some other form of ailment rather than a nervous disposition.

Todger was on a curfew while a patient in the hospital, but according to family, he often 'escaped' in order to see Robina Abram, the mother of his young son who had been born in 1915.

The vicarage was situated very close to the Cottage Hospital, which sat adjacent to it. It was the patients from the Cottage who had walked the short distance to the train station to welcome Todger's home from Euston to form his guard of honour.

On 31 January 1917, local man Samuel Johnson, who was a chemical labourer in Castner Kellner, was admitted to the Cottage Hospital with kidney disease. Johnson had pre-war service with the King's Liverpool Regiment, but he had been discharged as medically unfit. He had rejoined the colours when Britain declared war on Germany and had gone to the front with the Royal Garrison Artillery, but had been sent home on account of his poor health.

Johnson had then spent four months in bed at his home where his state of mind had begun to decline. On one occasion, he was found wandering aimlessly in the streets in his night attire and he had to be led back to bed. He was admitted to hospital in a state of severe depression.

As a patient, Johnson told the nurses that he wished he was dead. Several weeks after being admitted, in somewhat horrific circumstances, he got his wish. In a report following his death, it was recorded:

> Private Thomas Hawley, of the Border Regiment, a patient in the Cottage Hospital, said the deceased [Johnson] told him, on Sunday, that his mother was coming to see him in the afternoon. He asked him if he would shave him. Witness agreed and got his shaving tackle ready. He stropped the razor and put it on the locker between his bed and the deceased's. When witness had his back turned another patient called out, 'Look what he's doing!' and witness turned round and saw the deceased with the razor at his throat. He caught deceased's wrist and he dropped the razor.[11]

Pte Hawley snatched the razor away, but the damage had already been done. Johnson had slit his own throat and over the course of the next forty minutes, he slowly bled to death.

Todger may have been a hospital patient, but he was still fully mobile, and being a patient did not prevent him from being in great demand for public appearances. Many more were to come.

10

The Engagements Continue

On 1 December, mere days after being admitted to hospital, Todger travelled to Birkenhead to visit the regiment's HQ at Gamlin's Works where he had received his initial training back in 1914. He later attended a gathering in the council chamber at the town hall that was held in his honour, where he was welcomed by the mayor and Col. Lee, among others:

> The Mayor said Private Jones was the first member of the Cheshires to obtain the distinction, and they all rejoiced the honour.
>
> 'Todger' Jones then signed the visitors' book, and Colonel Lee, having expressed his thanks to the Mayor for the reception, the procession to headquarters was resumed amid cheers.
>
> On arriving at the headquarters of the 3rd Battalion at Laird-Street, Private Jones was received by the commanding officer, Colonel Gregg [*sic.*], with whom he had a private conversation.[1]

Incidentally, Col. Greg was the brother of Ernest Greg, whose son, Arthur, had led Todger in the Hill 60 bombing attack in May 1915 before being shot in the face. At this point, Arthur had recovered sufficiently from his wounds and was attached to the RFC, although he would be shot down and killed a few months later.

A large concert was held at the headquarters in the evening, and several presentations were made, including one from the sergeants of the battalion who issued Todger with an engraved silver cigarette case.

Todger returned home to prepare himself for yet another presentation that was planned for the following day. This time, it was at Runcorn's town hall, where an audience representing all sections of the town—political, religious, and social—were present.

To Todger's delight, the wounded soldiers from the hospital were sat in the front row. Todger himself was wearing his hospital blues for the event and had to leave early to meet his curfew.[2]

The ever-present Sir Frederick Norman presided over proceedings and Todger's parents were in attendance as honoured guests. The event began with the male-voice choir singing 'Rule Britannia', before Sir Norman—one never to turn his nose up at the chance to speak—provided the following words:

> We gather this afternoon to honour in tangible form a lad bred and born in our midst, a lad who has done valiant deeds which have touched the imagination of the Empire, a lad who has received direct from the hands of the greatest King on earth the highest honour a soldier can win. That is big stuff, and if you have gripped its import you will get away from the parish pump and realise that our lad won an outstanding place in national history. I frankly confess that the bigness of the business bothers me. My horizon stretches beyond the bounds of local circumstance to the setting which posterity will have for Private Jones, V.C. The day will come when the gold watch you gave him last Saturday 'will stop short, never to go again', when the address will fade, when these presents will go to rack and ruin, and I shall be surprised if in the meantime recognition of his valour does not take on some imperishable form, some day a statue of him will stand in our public place, and on its base will be emblazoned the names of those other heroes of ours who have bled for us and died for us in this war of liberty.[3]

Applause echoed throughout the hall at Sir Norman's rousing words.

He continued:

> The daring of his deed dazzles us; its strategy commands our admiration; its success makes the world wonder. Courage, coolness, resource—all the great qualities of a soldier—were there in superabundance. In that supreme moment of his life he flung all mortals hold dear on the altar of devotion to duty. What premium would an insurance agent have put on his life? What were the sporting odds against him? His comrades were sure that 'he had gone west', and a wire flashed to Princess-street would break the old hearts of his old father and mother. There were a million chances that he would be hurled into Eternity to the one chance that he would remain in Time. Thank God, Time won, and he stands today a peerless example of self-abnegation, that essential essence of Christianity of which we hear so much and see so little. Napoleon said that every private in his army carried a field marshal's baton in his wallet. Let us hope that Jones' brave heart, which to-day beats under a private's jacket, will some day throb beneath the tunic of an officer, and let Jones see to it that he qualifies like as regards honour and education for promotion if it comes his way.[4]

Sir Norman went on to explain that he was good friends with Rudyard Kipling's uncle, and that he would be relating Todger's deeds to him in the hope that Kipling would pen a poem to send Todger's exploits 'ringing down the ages'. 'Tennyson found his chance in "The Charge of the Light Brigade"', he told the eager audience, and 'Kipling can find his in the story of how Private Jones won the V.C.'[5]

The poem would never come to fruition, but others took up the challenge. One local resident penned the following verse:

Runcorn is smiling through its tears to-day,
Its clouds have vanished and the skies are blue;
For you have turned to brightness all its grey.
Brave 'Todger' Jones—the shouts are all for you.

Who but a Briton in this stress of shell
And lead torrential, ever charged so true
Up to the yawning, fiery gates of hell?
And you have charged and conquered, 'Todger'—you!

The happy townsfolk gather in their joy,
And all your way with flowers a welcome strew;
All faces beam with smiles for Runcorn's 'boy,'
And that is you, young 'Todger'—that is you.

A brazen prean hails you to your home,
The streets are gay with bunting—red, white, blue:
A swift pen writes down 'hero' in the tome
Of Runcorn's annals, and that hero—you.

Your deed shall live the pride of Runcorn's fame,
'The man whose strong right arm braved five score two
'Of William's best'; you earned a deathless name,
A soldiers glorious record, 'Todger'—you!

The 'cross' that dangles on your breast to-day
Tells all the best that human hands can do;
Now heaven returns you from the blighting fray,
That earth may shower its full awards on you.

War's furry failed to break you in your stride,
Failed to engulf you midst its drift and stones;
So now the old town's gates are open wide
To hail its hero, Private 'Todger' Jones.

A. J. Freeland.[6]

Tennyson or Kipling, the poet was clearly not; but the sentiment was there nonetheless. It is also a clear indication of the admiration and respect that Todger had garnered and of the interest that his deeds had evoked with the public.

In his speech, Sir Norman made mention of Todger's modesty and how he always spoke of his comrades while shunning the opportunity to speak of himself.

The chairman of the council, Mr. Smith, brought up Todger's health and frail appearance, and after seeing him in his red, white, and blue, he had 'began to think he had had enough of it, and if it went on much longer there would not be much left of him'.[7]

The audience had a good laugh at Todger's expense when the incident of him running away from the crowds was brought up by Mr Summerfield, a Conservative Party Politician and political opponent to the Liberals, who also gave his thanks for the invitation and for the 'broadmindedness; of inviting political opponents to the gathering'.

The press reported:

> [Summerfield] was glad to hear Todger mentioned for his modesty. He did not think there was any 'funk' about 'Todger' when he took 102 prisoners, but he thought there was a bit of blue funk or next thing to it when he came out of the station and saw, not enemies, but thousands and thousands of Runcorn friends. He thought his heart went pit-a-pat then, and if he dared with credit to himself as a soldier, have got out the back way he thought he would have done it. (Laughter.) Didn't he scoot down Back-High Street?—(Laughter.)—an when he got to his home he appeared at the bedroom window, and they had an example of the bravery and the modesty which always seemed to accompany bravery, for his first thought was for the lads in the trenches and the wounded.
>
> He believed they all recognized that the war was going on a great deal longer yet, and that the country was not really awake yet. Things happened in Runcorn, of course, but he did not believe that the country as a whole was really awake to the task. He fully believed that things were going to be much worse before they were better. If the war did any good it was in bringing to light noble deeds. Their townsman had won the highest honour the world could give to a soldier, and it was his pleasing duty to hand him the present. 'Todger' had been a member of the Liberal Club since he was a lad, and his old club pals decided to make him a presentation. The response exceeded their anticipations; men of all shades of opinion became associated. That was another pleasing thing that the war had done, it had united every one whatever their previous shade of politics was.[8]

The time then came for Todger himself to make a speech, followed by further words from his father, which brought applause from those in attendance:

Todger's Reply
An Appeal for his Pals

Jones, who was received with ringing cheers, said he was very glad to be with them once more, and to receive those gifts, for which he thanked them very sincerely. With regard to politics he thought the time had gone for that kind of thing, and they would all have to stand together if they wanted to win the war. The feeling that existed in the old days between Liberals and Conservatives had got to stop, and that was something for the chaps at home to do. They were doing their best perhaps in the factories and workshops, but they wanted to do more than that, and if they did not do it they would have to go through it when the lads came home. There were nearly four million lads out making sacrifices. Many of them had left wives and children, and others fathers and mothers. No one in England would ever know what they had gone through. They could see a little of it when they saw them in hospitals, some without an arm or a leg. What was going to become of them? Were they going to do something at once, or were they going to leave it as it was left after the South African War? It was up to the people who were left at home to see these men got justice, and not leave them to be a burden to someone. They ought to think these things out for themselves. They had a representative in Parliament who was supposed to think for them in Parliament, but so far as he (the speaker) was concerned he let none think for him. He could think for himself. (Laughter). They wanted to see that the Army at the front wanted for nothing either in food or ammunition. He asked that those who came home with one or more limbs short should be given a chance in life, and he would be happy. (Applause.)

At this stage Private Jones had to leave in order to be back in hospital by four o'clock.

A Father's Thanks

Mr. Jones, the V.C'.s father, expressed his thanks to the townspeople for the splendid reception they gave to his son on his arrival in the town, and also for the enthusiastic way they received him on that and other days. Both he and his wife felt a thrill of joy as they attended the enthusiastic gatherings which had been held to honour their son, who had fought well in the war. He also wished to thank Sir Frederick Norman very sincerely on behalf of himself and his wife for the excellent manner in which he had taken them through all they had to go. He must mention too the splendid generosity of the members of the Liberal Club, which they had shown in practical form, and but for the Army regulation they would have been only to glad to have done more.

He did not forget the men at the front, nor did any of them. They had done their duty, and some had been wounded and had not perhaps been honoured. He could assure them that so far as the townspeople of Runcorn were concerned

> they were appreciated for their valour in going out to defend the country from the barbarians, and those who would serve England as they had served Belgium if they had the chance. Were wars to go on for ever and ever? Was there no means of stopping them, with the horrible slaughter, wounding and hardships of trench life? In his opinion there were two ways which would stop war; one was arbitration, which, as some of them would remember, was adopted by Mr. Gladstone and America. The other way was by international union, under which all nations would be bound together with the object of refusing to allow any one nation to make war on another. He hoped the happy time would come when men would look upon one another as brothers, trying their best to serve one another, and not looking upon each other as enemy's.[9]

The text of the address from the Liberal Club following the presentation of his lifelong membership was as follows:

> Runcorn Liberal Club, Regent Street, November 9, 1916. To Private Thomas Alfred Jones, V.C.
>
> Dear Sir,—At the monthly meeting of the committee held on November 2nd the following resolution was adopted: 'It was unanimously decided to elect you a life member of the Liberal Club in commemoration of your attaining the distinction of the V.C. for conspicuous bravery in capturing single-handed 102 of the enemy in their trenches. It gives the committee great pleasure to confer this privilege, and the club members fully appreciate the honour of having upon its roll one who has so signally distinguished himself.[10]

A number of gifts were presented to Todger during the event. They included a case of cutlery and two framed photographs—one, a portrait photo of Todger; the other was of him marching at the head of his prisoners, but this photo is something of a curiosity. At the time, it was described as the 'official' image of Todger with his prisoners, and it was published in many papers up and down the country as such. The soldier leading the prisoners has what appears to be a bullet hole in his helmet, the position of which matches with the one from Todger's helmet. However, the soldier leading them appears to hold no resemblance to Todger, whose features are quite distinct.

That said, we do know that Todger was ordered to march his prisoners back for 'four or five miles', which gives ample opportunity for a photograph to have been taken. Alternatively, it is possible that the man was a 'stand in' for Todger and that once word of his exploit became known, it was deemed sensible to bag a photograph to celebrate the occasion, even if Todger himself was unavailable, as it was too good an opportunity to miss. As was proven, it was something that the press would lap up in earnest.

11

Back to the Front

Todger was eventually discharged from hospital, and he set out to rejoin his battalion. The Battle of the Somme had come to a close as Todger was receiving his VC, and the battalion had moved to billets at Le Touret before going into the line at Givenchy. They had been relieved on Christmas Eve, but 250 members of the battalion had been detailed to carry trench mortar ammunition on Christmas Day, which was probably the reason the battalion's 'Xmas Dinner' had been put on hold until January.

In April, Sam Poxon was wounded and left the battalion never to return, and later in the year, Todger received word that his brother, Arthur, had passed away on 30 July. After being wounded in October 1915, Arthur had spent three months in the North Western General Hospital in Hampstead where he underwent a major operation. Three further operations followed and, according to family, a metal plate was inserted in his skull.

He had been transferred to the Regimental Depot in April 1916 and was discharged from the Army in the June, 'no longer fit for war service', with a pension of 12*s* 6*d* per week. He had then gone to live with his parents who cared for him. Arthur evidently had the same fighting spirit as his brother. The following year, he gained employment as a 'weigher' at the local docks, but managed only a few weeks before having to quit. Pulmonary tuberculosis had developed through his hospitalisation, and he was in a weak state of health.

He became bedridden and contracted influenza. On the day of his death, he was the only adult in the house. His ten-year-old nephew, Charlie, was the only other person present, and he heard his uncle shouting for him. 'You had better fetch somebody,' Arthur had told him. Charlie ran to his Aunt Emily's house a little way up the street, but by the time they returned, Arthur was already dead.

Arthur had no children and was unmarried. He was buried with his sister, Lilly, who had died in infancy in 1879.

The battalion was in the front line and support trenches in the Oppy sector at the time, and Todger could do little else but carry on with the war.

Sadly, Arthur is not recorded as a casualty of war and, as a consequence, is not recognised by the Commonwealth War Graves Commission.

To Italy

In late 1917, Britain committed to sending a number of divisions to Italy, including the 5th, which departed from France on 12 December 1917.

Initially, the 5th Division was set to move into positions at Brenta, a mountainous area in the north-west region of the country, but the plan was changed, and they were sent to positions along the River Piave instead. Their time in Italy was entirely different to the trenches they were accustomed to on the Western Front, and the situation they now found themselves was more akin to peacetime. Not yet in the line, the men of the battalion had very little to do. They were put through a series of marches and some mild training, but their time was generally spent in a state of relaxation. Football matches were regularly played, no doubt much to the delight of Todger, whose prowess with the ball had earned him his earlier childhood nickname of 'Dodger'. In the words of the battalion history, this time was 'a very much needed change from the severity of the fighting in France, from which all ranks benefitted enormously'.[1]

Todger's quiet time in Italy gave way for reflection. On 1 February 1918, he wrote home to his parents venting his frustration of certain issues, showing a disdain for Prime Minister David Lloyd George—the reasons for which are not entirely clear:

> Dear Father & Mother,
>
> I hope by the time you receive this you both will be in the best of health, and the weather a lot warmer, especially for mother. The snow has cleared now, and the sun—when it breaks through—is lovely and warm, but it is still cold at night.
>
> I am the C.O's Orderly now: they made me take it. He's a Col. Roddy.
>
> We will be in the line when you receive this. It is quiet to what it was in France. I have had a crack with Mr. White's son to-night, and we think you are getting in a queer state in England as regards food. Do not send any more out here if it is like that. We are better off than you.
>
> I see Mr. Lloyd George, the wind-bag, has climbed down. It is through such pests as him that we are in this hole we are, and we have been prevented from winning. You, and a lot more I have spoken to as regards things in the War, will perhaps realise what I was trying to warn you about in 1915, 16 and 17. [People] will perhaps remember, and know they have been gulled. It may be

> hard for them to think so, but it has been a d--- [damn] sight harder for the few of us who are left, and had to keep on knowing it was only a mismanaged concern of popular ???, head office miles from the work, and is to blame for this terrible loss of life and money. Sometimes I feel that I couldn't face you, especially if it is going to be a patched-up Peace after the way thousands of the old boys have fought and hung on. I know that the spirit of my chums who are gone, would rejoice if they could see the three or four of us who are left, go through to final victory. But we are bound and helpless, and can only hope that God will give our country that which our long-range brainless leaders cannot conceive. Enough of this, eh?[2]

Todger went on to speak of his friends 'at the club', enquiring as to how they were getting on before asking his parents to pass on his thanks to 'Flo'—probably meaning his niece who was the daughter of his sister, Emily—who had sent him a letter.

Todger then reverted to a subject that he had first highlighted in 1916: the lack of leave for those who had been at the front for a long time. This was something that greatly frustrated him:

> There is not much chance of leave yet; we have had a draft of A.S.C. and the rotten authorities sent them to us, and they had not had leave for 18 months. It is a shame to do lads down of a chance to come home, after these people having three years in safety, and our boys going through hell. You at home ought to see the M.P's over such things, and want to know why so.
>
> I remain your ever-loving son,
>
> No. 11000, Pte. T. A. Jones, V.C.,
> 1st Cheshire Regt.
> B.E.F................Italy.[3]

Battalion HQ and two companies went into the front line for the first time on 10 February 1918. This coincided with the Regiment Day, or 'Meeanee Day'. In honour of the day, the battalion sent out a patrol that returned with a prisoner who had been snatched to 'celebrate the occasion'. The battalion's losses for the month of February were very minor and consisted of one officer and two men wounded. This was followed with three men killed and six wounded for the month of March. That same month, the Germans launched Operation Michael, their Spring Offensive on the Western Front. The attack succeeded in smashing through the Allied lines, and thousands of soldiers were put out of action, with many falling into enemy hands. The Cheshire Regiment's time in Italy came to an abrupt end. On 4 April, they boarded trains and began their journey back to France, where men were desperately needed more than ever.

In July, Todger was granted a period of leave. He returned home unannounced to find his parents were away on holiday but they were contacted by a wire and quickly returned home.

It was noticed that Todger looked much better and healthier than he did when last at home. The *Runcorn Weekly News* reported that he had put on weight and seemed to be much fitter than in November 1916.

Since his last leave, a tablet commemorating 'the greatest individual act of bravery of the war' had been installed in the drill hall. It had been unveiled earlier in the year in Todger's absence, during a modest ceremony that had involved various dignitaries and military personalities.

Todger went to see it and found it 'admirably designed and very artistic'.[2] Today, the tablet is located in the Cheshire Regiment Museum in Chester who relate that it came into their possession after it was pulled out of a skip and donated to them some years ago.

During his leave, Todger visited Chester where he once again spoke with the mayor, Sir John Frost, in his parlour at the town hall. A representative from the *Runcorn Weekly News* attempted to get further war stories from Todger and asked if they had been any recent happenings at the front, but Todger was reticent and had very little to say on anything to do with the trenches, and the reporter left without a story.

With his leave expired, Todger returned to the front. The battalion was in the front line at Le Sart in August where, on the 1st of the month, the Battalion HQ came under a violent bout of enemy shelling that resulted in just one man killed and another wounded. A further barrage, this time with gas, landed in the Battalion HQ area on the night of the 3rd, causing some twenty-two casualties to the 'other ranks', one of whom was Todger, who was temporarily blinded. He was admitted to hospital at Saint-Omer the following day, but he quickly recovered and was able to return to the battalion where he would soon be earning further recognition for his bravery.

Although initially very successful, the German Army's Spring Offensive eventually ran out of steam, and the opportunity to deliver a British and Allied counteroffensive that would ultimately win the war was promptly seized upon. This was the start of what would become known as the 'Hundred Days Offensive'. The proposal, put forward by the BEF's C-in-C Field Marshal Sir Douglas Haig to Allied Supreme Commander Ferdinand Foch came into play on 8 August with an attack at Amiens. German positions were overwhelmed along a 14-mile front, prompting German Commander Erich von Ludendorff to call it 'the blackest days for the Germany Army in the history of this war'.[4]

The Cheshires detrained from the Forest de Nieppe area on 14 August, and over the next five days, they marched to Bayencourt where they were involved in operations designed to cut off a considerable German force in the Ancre Valley. They moved to their assembly position west of Beugny village on 1 September, which they attacked the following day with the objective of capturing the village and occupying the high ground to the east on a 1,500-yard front.

As they formed up to advance, an immense barrage opened up, causing heavy casualties, particularly among the officers and NCOs, most of who were put out of action before the attack began.

Capt. Ferguson, who was wounded in the action, wrote in his diary: '… at 5 a.m. the enemy guns opened on our trench and in less time than it takes to write had just about blown us to hell'.[5] He continued:

> Great big shells fell right into our trench, causing at least 50% casualties before we started. We also got sneezing gas, and liquid fire was mixed up with H.E. [High Explosive].... Shells were now falling like hail and I saw a number of fellows blown to bits including two officers' batmen, who were just near me in the trench. A wounded runner came and gave me the Company roll, telling me it was from C.S.M. Smith who was wounded.[6]

Casualties among the battalion runners were also high. Two of them were blown up by a shell alongside Ferguson as they went to mount the parapet at the commencement of the attack.

'A' Company attacked on the battalion right. They went through the village and captured their objective, but after advancing around 1,000 yards, the left of the attack was held up by heavy machine-gun fire.

The Germans then launched an aggressive counterattack that pushed the left flank of 'A' Company out of the newly won trench. Men of the Norfolk Regiment who had attacked alongside them were also forced out of the position, but a British counterattack was immediately organised and pushed home to re-establish the gain.

Throughout the day, Todger acted as a runner. The space between the opposing trenches was swept by artillery fire but heedless of this, Todger made five journeys back and forth to deliver messages. He also rallied those who were lagging behind and led them forward into the enemy trench. The position was held through the night, the Germans retired, and the village remained in allied hands.

Todger's actions resulted in him being successfully recommended for the DCM. The DCM had been established in 1854 and, for other ranks, was second only to the VC. Earlier in the war, it had also been awarded for acts behind the lines, but discontent by those in the trenches had influenced a change of policy and efforts were made to ensure it went to fighting men only.

News of Todger's DCM filtered home the following month. Initial reports stated that he had been awarded it for the rescue of a wounded officer during a heavy barrage.[7] He may or may not have rescued an officer, but if he did, it was not recorded in the official citation:

> This man went forward five times with messages through an intense barrage. He also led forward stragglers and placed them in positions. His fine example and utter fearlessness of danger were a great incentive to the men.[8]

Decades later, during a 'Mons Day' reunion, Todger would modestly claim that he got it for 'just bits of jobs at Beaunay' when in actual fact 'the Regiment had lost many officers, and Todger noticed a number of men without orders and directions [and] led them to capture the enemy-held village'.[9]

His DCM was for an act far above what would have been expected of a private soldier. In leading forward a number of men and organising their dispositions, he had shown excellent leadership qualities and a complete understanding of the situation at hand. It is possible that Todger was still based at HQ acting as the colonel's orderly at the time. This would explain why he was selected to carry messages forward.

The Allied advance continued without pause. Miles of ground that had been under German occupation since early in the war was being taken back at a fast pace. German resistance was rapidly crumbling.

The Armistice

On the eleventh hour of the eleventh day of the eleventh month, the guns fell silent along the front. The war was over.

During Todger's time at the front, his mother had pleaded with him to keep out of harms way if possible and not to take any unnecessary risks. Her pleas had fallen on deaf ears, and Todger had refused to fulfil his mother's wishes. Now, he hoped she was glad that he had not shirked from danger.

In a letter to his mother at the time of the Armistice, Todger wrote:

> I am fairly well and will be alright in a day or two. With you, I thank God for his great care and guidance throughout this great struggle and I can now come home knowing that our cause has been right. When I meet you I can hold up my head proudly and say, 'We have won!' Many times you have asked me to keep out of danger if I could, but would you in your hearts, have liked me to have done so, are you not now glad that I didn't?[10]
>
> Our battalion took part in the last smash that made him throw in the sponge. And no wonder. It rained day and night for four days and we advanced about fifteen miles. Since 21st August we have won about eighteen decisive battles and advanced about ninety miles. It will be months before we come home as I think we are going to garrison a German town.[11]

Todger's comment about not getting home for a while would prove to be true. It would be many months before he returned to Runcorn.

Britain broke out into wild celebration when the Armistice was announced and towns and cities up and down the country rejoiced and partied at the news. Runcorn was no exception. Children were allowed to leave school early, and those at work were released for the day. People danced and sang in the streets.

Boats in the docks and on the canal sounded their horns. The entire scene was one of utter joy.

But while Britain celebrated wildly, for many in the trenches, there was nothing but a feeling of disappointment. This was not the victory they had expected and there was some resentment that they were not able to push home their victory all the way Germany.

Todger had mixed emotions when the Armistice arrived. The anti-climax gnawed away at him, and he felt the Germans should not have gotten off so lightly through the negotiated peace terms. He had no compassion for his enemy and felt the urge to punish them for causing misery upon many people, particularly those civilians whose sufferings he had personally witnessed.

Todger made his feelings known, venting his anger to his parents:

> We do not realise that the war is over yet, we took it very calmly and have not yet had the chance to celebrate our victory, not by anything with a bit of a kick in it. All the boys are sorry that we were not allowed to bring things home, that we were forced to halt and be robbed of the soldier's right of sacking and burning, as the Germans did in France and Belgium. Whoever is to blame made a great blunder as they do not understand the pigs and think they are lambs they are dealing with. I had a few lucky escapes on the last stunt. Private Evans has got the D.C.M. good luck to him. I suppose you know he was wounded. Tell his sister to let him know we are at Le Quesnay now, about midway between Valenciennes and Mons. We have been here for a week.
>
> It is pitiful to see the French prisoners coming back and seeing how their homes have been sacked. Some can hardly stand and look terribly thin and pale. In some of the villages we took the people were nearly frantic and they told us of the cruel way our prisoners have been treated. It has made us feel that we want to exterminate them.[12, 13]

Todger's comments about 'sacking and burning' may appear harsh, but he was a battle-hardened veteran whose sole focus for the past four years had been to destroy his enemy, and he wanted them to endure the war-ravaged suffering that France and Belgium had endured.

By now, those of the battalion who were present at the Battle of Mons back in August 1914 were few and far between. Nevertheless, the men of the battalion knew of what had happened and they were aware of the gallantry that had been displayed by those members of the battalion on that fateful day.

Mons had been occupied by the Germans since 1914. It was liberated on the last day of the war by Canadian forces, much to the delight of the inhabitants who had been under German occupation since the opening stages of the conflict.

Amazingly, news soon filtered through to the Cheshires that their miniature colour had survived undetected for the last four years behind enemy lines. Swift arrangements were made to retrieve it.

12

Return to Blighty

On 24 August 1914, the battalion had made a last stand at Mons while acting as rearguard, losing almost all of their number and ceasing to exist as a fighting unit.

When it had become clear that there was no way out, Drummer Baker had endeavoured to hide the battalion's miniature colour that had been placed in his care. With the Germans closing in, he had entered a building, rushed up the stairs, and hid the colour under the eaves behind some straw. Through frantic gesticulations he had communicated to the occupants that it was imperative that the colour remained hidden from the Germans. Baker had been captured shortly after leaving the house, but the story of the miniature colour had only just begun.

Pte Riley, who had been fighting alongside Baker, was aware of what Baker had done. Riley had been wounded during the battle, but he managed to escape the clutches of the Germans. He later reached a convent in Audregnies doubling up as a Belgian Red Cross Ambulance Hospital. While receiving treatment for his wounds, he confided in a sister and told her the story of the colour, impressing on her its importance and whereabouts. In turn, the sister had informed the Cure of Audregnies, M. C. Soudan, who took it upon himself to assist and to ensure the colour remained undiscovered. A cat-and-mouse chase then ensued.

Accompanied by the schoolmaster of Audregnies, M. Alphonse Vallee, and son-in-law of M. Matin, Soudan was able to remove the colour without detection and take it to his home where he kept it for some time until somewhere more secure could be arranged. Next, it was moved to the church and hidden behind one of the choir stalls, but this too would prove to be only a temporary measure. By November 1914, the Germans were stripping buildings of materials to use in their war effort, particularly cotton and copper. Soudan began to panic. Fearing the colour might be discovered, he acquainted M. Georges Dupont, the communal secretary, or town clerk, with the situation as it stood and of the subject of trust that had been laid upon him. It became clear that a safe place to hide the colour would be an extremely difficult thing to accomplish. Dupont then suggested that the colour be placed in the attic of the communal girl's school where his wife was the principal, which had no visible opening. It was taken to the school, bricked up, and completely concealed.

The precaution would prove to be vital. After a unanimous tip-off that the colour was hidden in the village, the Germans conducted a thorough five-day search in which every house was checked. The colour was not found, and nobody would admit to having any knowledge of its whereabouts. A reward of 2,000 marks was offered, but still no information was forthcoming. Those in the know had completely closed ranks. The colour would not be given up for any price.

It took more than four years, but the cherished colour was finally handed back to the battalion. On 15 November 1918, a party of men—headed by Capt. Sproule who, as a quartermaster, had landed with the original contingent in August 1914—travelled to Audregnies where they were told the colour was still bricked up behind a wall. Work began to extract it, and the next day the colour was finally handed over.

On 25 April 1919, a month before his demobilisation, Todger, who had recently arrived home after serving with the Army of Occupation, took part in a homecoming parade in Chester with Capt. Sproule and twenty-five other men.

Large crowds had gathered to see them and Sproule made a short speech, telling spectators that some 567 officers and 9,000 men had served in the battalion since August 1914. 'Some were still in the Army of Occupation,' he related, and 'others had been demobilised, and a great number had been left behind,' adding: 'On the day they had been longing for years, the day of their welcome home, they must remember the brave men they had left asleep under the ground 'in the little part of England over the water'.[1] Sproule, Todger, and the others were cheered as they marched to the Castle, especially the 'VC hero', Todger Jones.

The occasion was further enhanced by the presence of a sacred regimental heirloom—an heirloom that, through the profound efforts of a number of dedicated Belgian civilians, had survived the rigours of war and made it back to the home of the regiment in Chester. Todger was given the honour of carrying the miniature colour in the parade. It was an apt moment, with both man and colour representing the epitome, embodiment, and spirit of the regiment.

That evening, a dinner hosted by the mayor of Chester was held, where both Capt. Sproule and Todger gave speeches. Todger spoke of the Cheshires, saying 'that it was the regiment that had practically won the Mons ribbon for the whole of the Army'. He then directed his comments to the youngsters of the regiment who were present, telling them:

> I want you young soldiers—you band boys who are going to soldier on, always to have this in your memory. I know the Cheshires, and they never go back, and this division, the 5th Division, is the only division that has never retired since Mons.[2]

Todger went on to give a summary of the battalion's service in France, telling the audience that he felt the Cheshires on the whole were the 'finest regiment in the Army, and no other regiment could point to them and say they had lot an inch of ground during the whole war'.[3]

A Heavy Price

Runcorn was a small town with a small population, but the war had a massive effect on the inhabitants. Some 2,000 of its men folk served in the war, meaning one in nine of the town's inhabitants were in uniform. Almost 400 lost their lives and many more were wounded, with some destined to suffer lifelong crippling injuries. Hardly a street in the town had escaped loss in one way or another.

Princess Street was no exception. At No. 35, the Hallwood's lost both of their sons in the war. Sgt Thomas Hallwood had earned the DCM at Hill 60 in 1915 'when engaged in working underground [continually in water] preparing a mine which was successfully exploded', and he was also awarded the Russian 4th Class Order of St. George.[4] He lost his life on 12 April 1917, aged thirty-six. His brother, John, was killed on 9 August at Gallipoli, aged thirty-four. Both men had served with the South Staffordshire Regiment.

Then there was Arthur, Todger's brother, who had died in bed at his parent's home two years after being shot by a sniper on his first day in the trenches. Other family members also served, including a number of Todger's nephews.

While Todger returned to his job as a fitter and gelled back into civilian life with no apparent ill effects of his wartime experiences, others found the transition more of a struggle, particularly Todger's nephew, Joseph Edward Jones, who eventually returned to Runcorn a broken man.

Joseph had left England and sailed for Australia in March 1914, but shortly after his arrival, the war had broken out, and on 24 August 1914, he had enlisted in the Australian Imperial Force as a private in the 4th Battalion, 1st Infantry Brigade. He was twenty-one years old at the time and gave his occupation as a farm labourer.

He went to Egypt and then on to Gallipoli, landing on 25 April 1915, but just four days later, was shot in the right foot by a sniper and evacuated to a hospital in Cairo. He recovered and returned to Gallipoli, where he remained until the evacuation.

Joseph had then contracted influenza and spent the first two months of 1916 recovering before sailing for the Western Front with his battalion where they landed on 30 March. He was wounded again in July, this time severely, with a gunshot wound passing through his chest and back.[5] His condition was serious and it would be many months before he would physically recover. His mental wounds, however, would never heal.

On 12 September 1916, Joseph was shipped to England and admitted to York Hospital and later to the Lord Derby War Hospital. When discharged, he returned to duty, but his previously high standard of behaviour was now blemished with various instances of unauthorised leave and misconduct. He went absent without leave (AWOL) in December and again in February, forfeiting pay and spending time in custody.[6] For the latter offence, after being detained while awaiting trial, he was given a further thirteen days' detention on top of what he had already served.

Shortly after his last offence, Joseph was transferred to the 61st Battalion, but his behaviour continued its downward spiral. On 4 April, he went AWOL for six days and was given a lengthy detention and had his pay forfeited. Next, he neglected to obey rules and was found in an out-of-bounds area in hospital. He was quickly sent back to the 4th Battalion.

Joseph returned to Australia on 1 February 1918. He arrived the following month and received a medical discharge due to his wounds in the April.

Prior to the war, Joseph had planned on a new life in Australia, but the conflict had changed him and he decided to return to England to be with his family. His relatives recall him been hugely affected by his experiences, and it was common knowledge that he struggled to come to terms with what he had seen and endured. His niece, Anne Bamber, distinctly remembers Joseph having a hole in his body from a gunshot wound.

His transition was very different to that of his uncle's.

13

Post-War

Todger had returned from the war a hero and was instantly recognisable to everyone in his hometown. Despite this, he simply wished to get on with his life as it had been before. He returned to his work and continued to socialise in the local Liberal Club, playing darts and billiards and drinking with his friends.

As the recipient of a VC, he was in great demand for social events and was often invited to engagements both within the town and further afield. He enjoyed attending military events where he could mingle with his fellow soldiers. He attended the 1920 garden party at Buckingham Palace, at the request of King George V, which was held on the afternoon of 26 June. All recipients of the VC received invitations to the event, and there was an impressive turnout. The attendees assembled at Wellington Barracks before marching to the palace garden by way of Birdcage Walk, Horse Guards Parade, and The Mall. The VC men were headed by the band of the Welsh Guards who belted out their notes to the excited spectators. The king, who was accompanied by the queen, and various other members of the royal family, then inspected the recipients as they filed past him.

In 1925, Todger was a guest of honour during the king's royal visit to Runcorn. The two men had previously met at Buckingham Palace in November 1916 where the king had presented the Runcorn man with his VC, and both had also attended the 1920 Buckingham Palace garden party.

Todger was one of a number of honoured guests from Runcorn who stood in line to shake hands with the king. He stood between two other men, also renowned for their soldiering—Thomas Moffatt and Thomas Taylor, both of whom had fought at Rorke's Drift on 22–23 January 1879 during the Zulu War.

At Rorke's Drift, a garrison of approximately 155 men had fought off several thousand Zulu warriors from behind a hastily-erected defensive perimeter of mealie bags and biscuit boxes. The battle is one that is known throughout the world, not only for the eleven VCs that were awarded, but for the remarkable bravery displayed by both attacker and defender alike.

Moffatt and Taylor were both ex-privates from 'B' Company, 24th Foot, but the two men had not known that they were living just a stone's throw from one another. After it was announced that Moffatt would be a guest of honour at the royal visit and that he was a Rorke's Drift defender, Taylor had then come forward. He had moved to Runcorn from the nearby town of Hatton and his military service was not widely known beforehand, and he and Moffatt had not been aware of one and other.

Tom Taylor passed away in 1926, the year after the king's visit. Moffatt would live for another decade and was one of the last of the Rorke's Drift men to die, passing away in November 1936 at the age of eighty.

In her Rorke's Drift *Legacy* series, based on the lives of the participants of the battle, researcher and genealogist Kris Wheatley said of Moffatt: 'He was a tolerant man, but quite outspoken, he said what he meant, and he meant what he said, and [he was] a hard worker with a good sense of humour'.[1]

Moffatt had manned the north wall at Rorke's Drift, and it was here where the brunt of the Zulu onslaught was focussed and where much of the hand-to-hand fighting took place. In later life, he struggled terribly with what he had endured and is said to have suffered from reoccurring nightmares. On one occasion, believing he was under attack from his old enemy, the Zulus, he bolted from his home clutching one of his twenty-nine grandchildren in a bid to escape them.

Todger had been good friends with Moffatt. The wars of the two veterans had been very different—one involving Martini-Henry breach-loading rifle and bayonet against *assegai* and shield, and the other involving tanks, bombs, and artillery. Technological advances aside, the two men undoubtedly shared a bond. Both had certainly been through it, and it was not unusual for the townsfolk to see the two men together. Their favourite spot was a bench in the town, where they were often observed in deep discussion, no doubt putting the world to rights.

Both men possessed a fighting spirit and a determination to fight for their country, even in their later years. Todger would try his utmost to enlist in the Second World War, and Moffatt had done the same on the outbreak of the First World War. An article explaining Moffatt's determination featured in the *Runcorn Guardian* in May 1915, as well as his struggle to make ends meet:

> Moffatt is now verging on 60 years of age, but his family are quite young, and only one of the lads has left school and contributes towards the home. The veteran suffers from an enlarged liver following upon dysentery contracted in India, but is quite capable of light work. Unfortunately he did not serve the 21 years in the Army which was necessary for the gaining of a pension in his time.
>
> The fighting spirit is not dead within him, and he has thrice sought to enlist in Kitchener's Army, but, of course, has not been accepted.
>
> 'I feel I am able to do something,' he remarked, 'if they would only have me.'[2]

A local public subscription would bring some comfort and ease the pressure somewhat, but Moffatt, like many veterans, would continue to live a tough life on the breadline.

Another royal event, held by the Prince of Wales (future King Edward VIII of England), took place in November 1929. The prince had a great respect for the soldiers of the First World War. He had served with the Grenadier Guards during the war but, much to his chagrin, had been attached to the staff in a role behind the lines due to his royal bloodline. He had been awarded the MC in 1916 but was embarrassed by it.

The lavish reunion took place at the Royal Gallery in the House of Lords. In total, 319 recipients of the VC attended the event, including Todger. It was immensely popular with the public. It drew huge crowds and made national headlines. Many of those in attendance exchanged souvenirs, and items, such as napkins and menus, were signed by multiple recipients. Never one to turn his nose up at the chance of bagging a souvenir, Todger went one better and purloined a table cloth, which was signed by many of the VC recipients.

A surviving table plan shows that Todger sat at table No. 11, seat No. 335, between Maj.-Gen. Sir Owen Lloyd VC, KCB, who had earned his VC with the RAMC in Burma in 1893, and Company Quartermaster William Grimbaldeston, whose VC had come as a result of his actions at Passchendaele in 1917 while serving with the King's Own Scottish Borderers.[3]

Also present at the reunion was Hugh Colvin, the only other man belonging to the Cheshire Regiment to be awarded the VC.[4]

Over the years, Todger continued to make regular visits to his old school and he often found himself the subject of discussion among the town's youth. When pushed, he would speak of his experiences to enquiring children, and it was said that he displayed a good sense of humour about his younger days. He told some 'war stories' to his nieces too, telling them that he always made the effort to look after the youngest lads in his platoon, some of who, at seventeen and eighteen years old, were half his own age.

Liz Howard (*née* Fitton) was born in 1942 and lived a couple of doors down from Todger who at this point lived at No. 51 with his sister, Emily, and her family—their parents having passed away. Liz has vivid childhood memories of him sitting on an old kitchen chair on the front step of his house, 'watching children playing and the world go by'.[5] Liz's father, Les, would often stop and chat with Todger. Both played the piano, and Todger told Les that he enjoyed listening to him play as he sat on his chair on the street.

It was a close-knit community. Next door to Todger lived the Shaw family, and Olga, also born in 1942, would nip in to see Todger and Emily almost every day, and Todger would let her play his old piano. Olga also enjoyed seeing the 'pretty back yard', which Todger was very proud of. Other properties on the street had tin baths hanging on the wall by the toilet, with dolly-tubs and large roller-mangles and other necessities. Olga recalls that Todger's yard was 'different':

> There were tubs of colourful flowers, and a stone bird bath bringing a touch of well deserved luxury into the life of a man who had seen so much death and destruction, and who had saved the lives of hundreds of his comrades by his total disregard of danger.[6]

Despite Todger's pleasant and peaceful activities in post-war years, the fighter within him would never leave. He had always been a tough lad. He stood for no nonsense and any argument was more often than not settled by the use of his fists. Percy Dunbavand, Todger's nephew, remembers 'Uncle Tom' and his friends, including William Allaby who was subsequently killed in the war, hiring a horse and cart on which they made their way though the towns of Frodsham and Helsby on their way to Chester for a drinking session. Somewhere along the way, Todger picked up a kitten, which he took, or attempted to take, with him on the journey. A man confronted him about it, and things turned violent. The man was knocked senseless by Todger, who then ended up in court over the assault.

In 1939, on the outbreak of the Second World War, Todger tried and failed to enlist into the infantry. He was far too old and could not be accepted. Instead, he became an air raid warden in Princess Street, and a member of the Home Guard. He patrolled key areas of Runcorn, including around the post office in Runcorn High Street, and at the Runcorn railway bridge, where he would check papers and IDs and refuse access when the air raid sirens sounded.

It was a cause of humour that Todger, owing to a shortage of weaponry, was issued with a broom in place of a rifle when drill inspections were carried out. For the man who was once renowned for his shooting skills, this was quite a come down, but Todger was just happy to be doing his bit.

Todger was a regular visitor to the regimental barracks, and he was regularly invited as a guest of honour to their functions. In an event held at Chester Castle, he was on hand to see the regiment return from their three-year stint in the Middle East in 1954.

When the discussion turned to his VC, which it invariably did, Todger would always play down his heroics and make light of what he had done. During one of his visits to Chester, Todger spoke to an individual who was employed by the regiment, saying that he 'did not know what all the fuss was about' as he had 'only captured an aid post'.[7]

The White Flag

Todger's 'off the cuff' comment about capturing an aid post is extremely intriguing, and it throws up some very interesting possibilities.

The citation for Todger's VC states that he shot a sniper who was taking shots at him. It then goes on to say that he spotted 'two more of the enemy firing at him, although displaying a white flag'.[8]

Todger, however, described seeing the white flag as he was digging in, which was prior to him going over and shooting the first sniper. Somewhere along the way, the sequence of events was slightly muddled.

Questions will forever remain unanswered. Was the white flag being displayed by the snipers or by some wounded men who were perhaps wanting to surrender but just so happened to be in close proximity to the snipers? Todger and his comrades of course would not have known whether or not this was the case and would have naturally suspected foul play.

White flag 'incidents' were a common occurrence through the war. They were not at all one-sided. Accusations of misuse were thrown back and forth, particularly in the earlier stages of the conflict, before movement on the field was replaced by trench fighting.

At least one member of the 1st Cheshires had found himself in a spot of trouble during their epic Mons action. The man in question, Pte Harrison, had found himself in danger of being shot by a group of Germans who had captured him and accused him of shooting at them while flying the white flag.

Harrison explained to his captors that it had in fact been the building next door to the one he was firing from that had been flying the flag and that he had not surrendered at the time and was not personally displaying the flag. Incidentally, the building next door was being used as a dressing station.

The timely intervention of a German officer had defused the situation and Harrison—who was on the verge of being shot on the spot—escaped with his life, albeit with a bayonet wound to his face that had been inflicted before the German officer had intervened.

Situations like Harrison's were commonplace, and in the heat of battle, it was often impossible to know for sure if any act of treachery had occurred. There are almost certainly instances where the white flag was misused, but there were also many occasions where it was believed to have been misused when in actual fact it was not.

Since the opening stages of the war, newspapers back in Britain had been seizing any opportunity to stir up the patriotic public with stories of their barbaric enemy. Stories of German atrocities both on and off the battlefield were widely published. It mattered little whether or not those stories were true.

One unfortunate incident occurred on 14 September 1914 during the Battle of the Aisne, when the Coldstream Guards, together with some men from nearby units, had forced the surrender of a body of Germans, numbering approximately 150, who had been almost completely cut off and outflanked. Having observed their enemy throw up their hands and begin to move towards them in surrender, the British also began to move forward with the aim of meeting them and accepting the surrender. But as they advanced, the British found themselves under a heavy fire from other Germans on the flank who were still fighting. Things quickly became confused. Seeing that the British who were to take them prisoners were now incapable of doing so, those Germans who had 'surrendered' changed their mind and once again took up the fight. One unfortunate British soldier who was wounded during the incident said they where 'simply mowed down' and related that 'not a single one of [them] walked off the field'.[9]

At the time, the press reported that the troops were the victims of a ruse and that the Germans had purposely lured the British into a false sense of security before springing their pre-planned trap.

However, after the war, when compiling the regimental history of the Coldstream Guards, their CO, Lt-Col. Sir John Ross, admitted he was very sceptical of the accusations:

> There were several of these instances during the first few months of the war and, as it was believed at the time that they were due to treachery on the part of the Germans, there was much indignation that so unworthy a trick should be resorted to by a belligerent. While this might have been the case in some instances, it is quite possible that no treachery was intended. White flags displayed in an unauthorized way by a few men cannot cause the fire to cease on the whole battle-field, and men who leave their cover under such circumstances run the risk of being shot down by friend and foe...[10]

Fast forward two years to September 1916 at Morval on the Somme and the same caveat applies. Enemy soldiers in one particular position intent on surrender does not mean the entire German line wished to do the same.

Did the sniper wave a white flag while firing, or was it was actually someone else who was nearby? If the latter, were those who wished to surrender wounded? None of the questions in this white flag conundrum will ever be answered, and, with exact specifics being somewhat obscured, the jury must remain out on the precise circumstances of the flag.

Whatever the case, none of this detracts from Todger's bravery, which cannot be disputed. His casual remark about it being an aid post is perhaps typical of a man who made a habit of talking down his own actions. In all probability, having just come through a battle, there would have been some wounded among his prisoners.

Todger charged an enemy position alone and accounted for the enemy snipers before taking on at least another eight German soldiers intent on killing him once he had entered their trench, so it is evident he encountered Germans who had no plans of surrender.

His remark, made years after the event, may be a case of simple modesty—making light of his achievements as he so often did. Alternatively, there is a possibility that some of the dugouts did contain some wounded men.

It is also worth highlighting that the photograph of Todger at the head of his prisoners—if, indeed, it is what it purports to be—shows them walking unaided with no apparent signs of wounds.

14

Family and Personal Life

In the past, there has been an element of reluctance to speak of certain aspects of Todger's personal life. This hesitancy to divulge information is perhaps understandable, but as time goes by, and attitudes progressively relax, information once deemed delicate in nature is no longer seen as such and things that were once brushed under the carpet are now discussed openly between family members and indeed further afield.

On 8 April 1915, while on the Western Front, Todger became a father to a little boy called Thomas William Jones Abram. Prior to the war, Todger had relations with a young lady called Robina Abram who was born in the first quarter of 1895. She was fifteen years Todger's junior and still in her teens when she became pregnant with Todger's baby. This occurred around the time of the outbreak of the war, which possibly impacted their relationship.

Although their relationship did not flourish, there is little doubt that Todger and Robina held strong feelings for one and other. The family relates that, during his time as a hospital patient following the award of his VC, Todger plotted a number of 'escapes' by climbing from a window after his curfew in order to visit Robina.

Todger remained a bachelor all his life, but it would seem that at one point, he and Robina did come close to marrying. Paul Smitham, Todger's paternal great-grandson, explains:

> My Grandmother told me that Todger would sneak out of Hospital to meet Robina Abram. My Grandad would have been born then and I'm led to believe that they planned to marry. I don't know if it's true but I have be informed that the Army and the Runcorn town Clerk stopped this from happening as VC heroes don't wed unmarried mothers. Gran said Robina's mother and Todger's mother hated each other with a vengeance. On that day when Todger came

> home to Runcorn to his heroes welcome Robina's mother held my 18 month old Grandfather aloft yards from him and yelled 'You've had you glory Todger, now here's your shame.'[1]

Following his leave and subsequent recovery from his ailment, Todger returned to the war. Meanwhile, around the time of the Armistice, Robina married Joseph Griffiths who lived locally and was the same age as her and together they raised Robina's and Todger's son. Joseph died in 1962 and Robina in 1983.

Robina was already married by the time Todger returned from service. She took her husband's name and became known as Robina Griffiths, but young Thomas retained his double-barrelled birth name of Jones-Abram.

Sadly, although he would pay maintenance for his son until he reached working age, Todger had no contact with young Thomas, and nothing was ever openly said on the matter.

However, young Thomas grew up amid rumours and he knew that Todger was his father, but Todger's family would remain silent on the subject. Todger's sister, Emily, would deny that her brother had a son at all.

In later life, Thomas Jnr was employed as a crane driver. He went on to marry Minnie 'Min' Edna Nash. They led happy lives and in time raised their own family. Thomas served in the Royal Navy during the Second World War, serving a total of five years from January 1941 to January 1946 before been discharged to Class 'A'. His certificate of service shows that, at just 5 feet 4 inches, he was relatively short in height, although, like his father, he was certainly not one to be messed with.

Thomas did not speak to his family about Todger. The subject was never really broached for the simple reason that no one dared to ask. On one occasion, a customer in the local British Legion where Thomas was working behind the bar dared to ask the prying question. The man later woke up on the floor of the club, after being knocked out cold by Thomas. It is perhaps little wonder that the subject was largely ignored.

In all their years of marriage, Thomas only mentioned Todger to his wife, Minnie, on two occasions, and these, as explained by his grandson, Paul Smitham, occurred several decades apart:

> I remember my Gran saying Grandad only mentioned Todger to her twice in their life; when they first met, and about a year before he died when he said out of the blue, 'I'm going to try to claim my Dad's VC.' He did start proceedings but fell ill and passed away.[2]

Another story, again related by Paul Smitham, refers to Todger's funeral. After making contact with, and speaking to, some of Todger's relatives who had attended it, Paul explained:

> They said that there was a man there that they didn't know on his own but who had a strong family resemblance. They approached the man and asked him who he was. They said he stormed off looking annoyed and they never got to know who the man was. I believe that man was my Grandad.[3]

Shortly after Todger's death, his sister, Emily Lightfoot, donated her brother's VC and the majority of his other medals to the Cheshire Regiment. Interestingly, since she had always denied that her brother had a son, Emily handed Todger's Liberal Club Medal to Robina, presumably so she could pass it on to Thomas when she saw fit.

Paul Smitham relates that 'she had the medal hidden away for years. Then, just before she died she gave granddad the medal in 1983. I don't know why she left it all those years; she must have had it since the 1950s after Todger died.'[4]

Todger lost three of his brothers between 1923 and 1926, and, of course, Arthur had died in 1917 and his mother, Elizabeth, passed away in 1927, having been unwell for some years. She died in her bed at home following an accident in somewhat sad circumstances. Todger, who was still residing with his parents, was present at the time of his mother's death and had done all he could to help her. He described the circumstances of her death during the inquest that was held following her demise, the details of which were subsequently published:

> Mrs Elizabeth Jones, mother of 'Todger' Jones, Runcorn's V.C. met her death under distressing circumstances on Monday morning. The old lady, who lived with her husband and son at 39 Princess Street, was well known in the locality. The circumstances surrounding her death formed the subject of an inquest on Tuesday morning, when Lieutenant-Colonel Ridgway attended at the police buildings.
>
> Mr Edward Jones, the widower, said his wife was 79 years of age. The old lady, he said, had been in failing health for the past seven years and during that period had frequently been attended by the doctor. Her condition gradually became worse, and on Thursday August 25th, Doctor Rooke was again called in. Subsequently she appeared to improve, and about six o'clock on Monday morning of this week she said she felt a little better and had had a 'fair night'. When getting out of bed she appeared to faint, and in falling caught a small table with her face. Their son came upstairs and put his mother back in bed. She was bleeding slightly, but appeared to revive after a little whisky and water. The doctor was summoned, and after his visit she appeared to go to sleep. Later in the morning he was informed she had passed away.
>
> Todger Jones V.C., the old lady's son, told the coroner that he took up a cup of tea to his mother about 6-50 on Monday morning. She then told him she had had a fairly good night. Twenty minutes later he heard a crash, and on going up stairs found his mother lying on the bedroom floor. He put her into bed and sent for the doctor, but he could do nothing for her, and she passed away about 9-30 AM.

> Doctor Rooke said he had attended Mrs Jones for the past two and a half years. He was called in early on Monday morning and was informed she had had a fall. The old lady was very poorly and was suffering very much from shock. In his opinion death was due to the shock caused by the accidental fall.
>
> In returning a verdict in accordance with the medical opinion, the coroner said he was quite satisfied that the members of the family had done everything they possibly could for the benefit of the old lady. It was an unfortunate happening, and he expressed his sympathy with the relatives.[5]

Todger's father outlived the majority of his children, dying in 1932 at the grand old age of ninety. Percy Dunbavand, Edward's great-grandson, remembers going to visit him shortly before he passed away as he lay gravely ill in his bed. Although just four years old, Percy distinctly remembers climbing the hard carpet-less stairs on his hands and knees. Upon entering the room, Percy saw his great-granddad who 'had a great grey beard and piercing eyes'. Edward was a tough man, and he looked it right until the end.

Todger Passes Away

In 1954—at which point he was seventy-three years old and living with his sister, Emily, at No. 51 Princess Street—Todger attended the regimental 'Mons Day' at The Dales. It was said he had missed previous Mons Day reunions, 'partly because of ill-health due to his being gassed' in the war.[6] It was said that he was slow to talk about his experiences in the war, but after a while, he gave in and began to speak. It was during this event that he admitted that he did some things that he really should not have done and the story of the eighteen-year-old runner being killed at Morval was also brought up. Todger then gave a brief account of that day, summed up in a few sentences, of how he had captured the prisoners. This would be the last event he would ever attend.

On 4 January 1956, Todger was admitted to the Runcorn Victoria Memorial (Cottage) hospital with heart trouble. He remained a patient until passing away on the afternoon of 30 January. The causes of death were given as pulmonary embolism, auricular fibrillation, and arteriosclerosis. His niece, Florence 'Flo' Anderton, who was the landlady of The New Inn where Todger regularly drank, was the informant when his death was registered.

Runcorn was plunged into grief at the news of Todger's death. Not only was he extremely well-known for his battlefield heroics, but he was also a hugely popular man through his many social circles and his large extended family. Everybody in the town knew Todger Jones.

Flags at the town hall and parish school, where he had attended as a child and to whom he had regularly returned to present awards, were flown at half-mast as a mark of respect.

Todger was buried in Runcorn Cemetery. The *Runcorn Weekly News* reported on his graveside funeral service:

> To show their sense of bereavement, the townspeople, young and old, lined the whole route as the cortege moved from the home in Princess Street—where he lived with his sister—to St. Michael's Church where there was a congregation to take part in the service. The coffin, draped in the Union Jack, was surmounted by a cushion upon which lay the military medals of this 76-year-old [*sic.*] soldier, including the Victoria Cross.[5]

At the service, Reverend Good, the chaplain to the Runcorn Branch of the British Legion, said:

> Those of us, who knew Tom Jones, knew him as a kindly and quiet man—a retiring sort of fellow, never willing to put himself into the limelight. He always thought of himself last. Knowing that, we can understand how it was that in the First World War he won the supreme honour of the V.C.[6]

At the time of Todger's funeral, Bill Raftery was a seven-year-old schoolboy who attended Victoria Road School situated beside the cemetery. After providing the pupils with a brief account of Todger Jones and his deed, the teacher directed them to the row of windows on the top floor to watch the proceedings.

A number of distinct memories of the occasion have remained imprinted in Bill's memory, including the sight of the chaplain who was dressed all in white facing the coffin that was draped in the Union Jack. Things took a turn when a number of soldiers fired a succession of shots into the air. This startled the children and caused the girls to shriek and cry in terror. The pupils were quickly ushered away from the window, although they were allowed to return once the shooting had stopped.

As previously mentioned, Todger's sister, Emily Lightfoot, presented her brother's war medals to the regiment after his death. They were received by Col. B. Y. Hayes-Newington, secretary of the Regimental Association, on 15 May 1956. Hayes-Newington accepted them on behalf of the regiment and, in return, he presented Emily with a brooch in the design of the badge of the regiment.

Todger's Territorial Force Efficiency Medal, George VI Coronation Medal 1937, and Elizabeth II Coronation Medal 1953 were not donated.[7] A photograph of Todger in his Home Guard uniform shows him wearing all of his medals. Mounted together on a bar are his VC, DCM, 1914–1915 Star, British War Medal, and Victory Medal. All of these medals relate to his First World War service and were given to the museum. The others—that were not donated—can be seen pinned loosely below those that directly relate to his war service. These medals still reside with the family.

Several other medals and medallions also remain with the family. After the war, the Liberal Club presented each of its members who had contributed to the war effort with a medallion in recognition of their services. These were presented during a social evening held in 1920 when some forty veterans were in attendance to receive their token of gratitude from the club. Sir John Brunner hosted, and Sir Frederick Norman made the presentations. Six medallions were presented to the families of those in the club who had paid the ultimate price. One of them went to the Joneses for Arthur who had been killed. Todger received a medallion and a gift of £41 from Sir Frederick Norman. He then gave a short address, urging his fellow Liberals to work towards helping and assist those who had suffered and were continuing to suffer as a result of the war.

15

A Character Assessment

We are lucky to have a wealth of material relating to Todger showing just what type of soldier and man he was, not only from the abundance of written sources, but from those who personally knew him.

At the time of his VC, the regimental journal described him as 'salt of the earth'. Todger truly was a great favourite with his comrades and this is testified in letters and articles that date before his VC act, proving that he was highly thought of prior to his elevation to national hero and that the words of praise did not merely come as a result of his award.

He was a humorist and a joker, and he took it upon himself to look after the younger lads. He was extremely brave. Not only that, but he also showed excellent leadership qualities and was at ease making decisions and advising those of higher rank on their best course of action. The NCOs looked to him for guidance, and he was happy to give it, as was the case at Hill 60 when an NCO had turned to him to lead them out of the bombing fight. On coming through the heavy fighting at Falfemont Farm on the Somme in which Todger and his fellow bombers played a lead role, it was he who had volunteered to assist men from another unit who had been without water for more than two days. This was despite him just coming out of battle and being exhausted and battle weary himself.

Todger's actions that earned him the DCM were also above and beyond what would be expected of a private soldier. Attacks and counterattacks were taking place, and some men found themselves without officers or orders. Todger made repeated trips through heavy barrages to deliver messages after other runners had been hit. He was able to take stock of the situation, rally those 'stragglers', and lead them forward 'to capture the enemy-held village'. Not only that, he then had the skill and confidence to place the men into strategic positions—evidence, if it were needed, that he was a solid and confident leader of men.

In a speech following Todger's VC, Sir Frederick Norman addressed the crowd. During his speech, Norman expressed his hopes that 'Jones' brave heart, which to-day beats under a private's jacket, will some day throb beneath the tunic of an officer…'[1]

Sir Norman's wish, spoken to a room full of people in Runcorn, received a round of applause from the audience. One can picture Todger smiling as Norman made the proclamation, taking it gracefully in the good spirit it was intended, but Todger's ambitions did not match Sir Norman's enthusiasm. Todger was no officer and certainly no 'gentleman'. He was a working-class lad through and through, and the 'temporary gentleman' status of wartime officer did not suit him one bit. Todger did not receive a single stripe for the duration his active service.[2]

Some old soldiers simply were not cut out for promotion, but many who were did not always step up. There are a number of reasons why these worthy and completely capable individuals did not rise above the rank of private.

Like Todger, Frank Richards was an old-hand and a highly decorated soldier whose time in the Army saw a distinct lack of promotion come his way. Richards, a regular soldier of the Royal Welsh Fusiliers with many years experience who had both the DCM and MM to his name, held the view that 'any old man could have been given a stripe or two if he wanted them'.[3]

In his war memoir, *Old Soldiers Never Die*, Richards wrote that 'many did not wish to take the leap from private soldier to NCO [while] others knew they held all the cards and, for the "old hands" promotion was readily available at a rapid speed'.[4]

It essentially boiled down to whether or not the particular old hand wanted a promotion. Richards cited one of his friends as an example, who, on a number of occasions, had refused to make the leap from private to lance-corporal after being asked to do so by his superiors. After eventually agreeing to take promotion, Richards's friend had told his officer that he would agree to become a sergeant 'or nothing'. He duly got his promotion, thus gaining three stripes in one fell swoop. Such was the need for good experienced NCOs.

The British Army was often in desperate need of quality NCOs. John Lucy, who began as a private and ended the war as an officer, thought 'the non-coms were very poor stuff'.[5] Christopher Stone, DSO, MC, an officer with the Royal Fusiliers, agreed with Lucy's assessment, claiming in 1917 that 'the men are first rate, though the NCOs are rather weak'.[6]

Many experienced privates were far better soldiers than some NCOs, and they could have filled the roll admirably, but many refused to entertain it, and many young and inexperienced conscripts often found themselves fulfilling the role, in charge of men twice their age with years of wartime experience behind them.

In his book, *Johnny Get Your Gun*, John Tucker describes being approached about him becoming an NCO. Tucker wrote: 'I did not want promotion … preferring freedom when off duty. I had noticed that our corporals seemed to have a pretty thin time, getting frequent extra work ... and [they] appeared to be used as general dogsbodies'.[7]

Frank Richards had similar thoughts. 'I had refused promotion many times,' he wrote. 'I should have been on parade day and night ... if I had been an N.C.O.... But, as it was, every morning the officer would inspect the billet and then I was free to go scrounging around.'[8]

John Lucy, when writing about peacetime promotions, went further in highlighting the pitfalls of taking a stripe or two:

> Work increases, and the young non-commissioned officer is kept busy from morning until night, ordering out routine parties for parades and fatigues, or looking after a barrack-room of soldiers some of whom are old enough to be his father.[9]

Lucy considered 'the first step from the ranks ... the hardest to bear'.[10] When he took the leap, Lucy felt 'a queer shame', knowing that the 'idea is scorned by the ordinary, professional, long-service private'.[11]

> A newly-made lance-corporal can be the unhappiest man in the army. He is immediately isolated from his old companions, and his new friends jealously watch him for any faults, while the single chevron which marks his rank usually numbs his brain; the little strip of cloth appears to be of huge dimensions, and its wearer to be the cynosure of all eyes....
>
> It is an acid test indeed, and personality is developed and character formed in seeking a nice balance of behaviour impressive both to the men and the senior N.C.O.s.[12]

It also bothered Lucy that officers 'were always ticking them off and warning them against familiarity with the men, whom they called by their Christian names'.[13]

These NCOs may have done the job during the rigours of everyday trench life and when out of the line completely, but when the fighting started, the old soldiers came into their own.

Todger was not one to order his mates to do as he said. They would look to him for guidance and leadership whether he had a stripe or not, chiefly in battle or in other times of danger, such as enduring enemy artillery. However, to be an NCO meant upholding strict standards whether in or out of the line, and this was far from Todger's style. He thought the world of his comrades, and he wanted to serve with them, not above them. He was not one to volunteer himself for more responsibility when out of the line, but when the fighting started, he became a leader. At least one contemporary newspaper report claims that Todger had once taken command of a whole company when in action, although this may not be completely accurate, as a company would consist of a number of platoons, each with its own officer and NCOs.

Todger could almost certainly have taken a promotion if he desired it. He had a cool head in a crisis and was a seasoned soldier. He was also highly decorated, and when a man was decorated for his gallantry, promotion often followed.

Many seasoned soldiers who eventually did take promotion often realised it was not for them and reverted back to their old rank at their own request. Others were demoted for their behaviour. It was not uncommon to see a private promoted to lance-corporal on more than one occasion only for them to be busted back down again for some offence, varying in its severity, but often being no more than a petty misdemeanour that many old hands were guilty of from time to time.

Todger's record shows that he did not gain any promotion only to lose it again, nor was he in trouble very often. Apart from a stint of field punishment (No. 1) for overstaying his leave over the Christmas (and his birthday) period, nothing else is noted on his record. He admitted that he did some things he should not have, but these must not have been serious enough to warrant formal punishment. He was more of a 'character' than a badly-behaved soldier, although it is said that he was 'a regular recipient of the nastier work details for disciplinary reasons'.[14]

Interestingly, in his book *Awarded for Valour*, Dr. Melvin C. Smith writes that Todger, on the day of his VC act, had been detailed to empty 'honey tubs' from the company latrine when the sniper began to shoot. Smith writes that a friend from his hometown of Runcorn was then shot and killed beside him and it was this that had prompted Todger to go out on his one-man attack. On the surface, this would seem improbable. The company had only just taken the village and were in the process of digging in on its outskirts, as confirmed in official documentation. Quite how and why they would have dug (and subsequently filled) latrines before digging a basic trench is confusing to say the least.

The act that earned Todger his VC was brought about following his disregard for a direct order issued to him. He had been told more than once to continue digging, and that he was not to attack or leave the position. The German soldiers were experts in counterattack, and many newly-won positions were lost by their swift counters. At Morval, the officer was following his own orders to consolidate as quickly as possible, hence he sternly told Todger to do as he was told. Men have been court-martialled or landed themselves in bother for much less. It is interesting to consider what would have happened to Todger if he returned empty-handed from his foray into the German line. It is easy to punish a man who achieves nothing after disobeying an order, but it is decidedly more difficult to punish one who returns with over 100 prisoners.

There is often a fine line between a heroic act and one that lands the individual in trouble, and men who are prone to being a thorn in the side of their superiors are often the same men who excel in battle.

Despite some minor niggles, there is no question that Todger was a fantastic soldier to have by your side. As a territorial, he was described as a model soldier who was well-known, not only for his fine marksmanship and soldierly qualities, but also for his smartness. So why did Todger remain a private soldier through the entire war? In short, he was one of the boys, and he simply would not have it any other way.

Todger was undoubtedly proud of his awards, but from his comments, he clearly believed the system was flawed with many deserving soldiers not being given the recognition they deserved. In a war where, on a regular basis, men overcame their fear and advanced into a storm of metal and where self-sacrifice was common, Todger struggled to see his own efforts as any more deserving than many other acts of courage he had witnessed. This is possibly why he found the public adulation embarrassing, why he played down his exploits, and why he championed the plight of others. He would see friends and family lost to the lottery of chance, where luck determined whether bullet or indiscriminate flying shrapnel would kill or maim. He would experience both horror and adrenalin-rush of battle, and endure and overcome the numbing fatalism particular to those fighting and surviving in the trenches. He was to travel a harrowing path along which many others failed to survive. He would soldier on, sustained by his maturity and self-confidence that never became hubris. Indeed, humility and humour were his backbone, and for his comrades, an empathy for their suffering was foremost. He would prove to be a hard man, sustained on his path with aggression, born from his belief in the justice of the cause and his natural soldier's instinct. The core that made him what he was and would become could be described as personal pride, but it is probably better described as 'bloody mindedness'.

16

Remembrance

In March 1918, a tablet was unveiled in Runcorn 'to ensure that generations to come shall know of the fame and courage of 'Todger Jones…'[1]

The tablet was presented to the drill hall by the Runcorn Urban Council on behalf of the subscribers and the Cheshire Territorial Association was entrusted with its care. Those present on the platform during the occasion included Mr. A. T. Smith (chairman of the Runcorn Urban Council), Sir Frederick Norman, Mr. and Mrs. S. Taylor, Col. Thompson (secretary of the Cheshire Regiment Association), Col. Saner, Maj. Ashton, Maj. Timmins, Lt Bourne, and several others. Todger's parents were also present, so too was a detachment of the local Volunteers under Lt Mayston and Lt Beck.

During the ceremony, Maj. Timmins told those in attendance that '15 months had elapsed since Runcorn was electrified by the news that one of her own townsman had won the coveted honour of the Victoria Cross, the decoration that was awarded only for the most conspicuous bravery and distinction in the presence of the enemy'.[2]

He went on to add further recollections, including the humorous moment during Todger's coming home parade where he had 'done a runner':

> All would remember how Runcorn went mad with enthusiasm on the day that Private T. A. Jones V.C., came home. He had testified as to how embarrassed he was by the wealth of his reception, and what a relief it was to see, outside the station, a bit of khaki that included some of his old chums and convalescent soldiers. They would also recall the resource he showed in bolting down a side street and arriving at his own base in a very short time.[3]

Those who had gathered for the occasion laughed as they remembered Todger swiftly dashing away from the crowds in order to reach the sanctuary of his home.

The drill hall also had a wall plaque naming those Runcorn men who had served in the Second Boer War, which had been unveiled on 26 June 1901. Maj. Timmins now said he hoped a 'permanent memorial' would also be installed in the hall to record the names of all those men who had served, or who were serving in the present war.

The tablet dedicated to Todger now resides in the Cheshire Regiment Museum in Chester. According to staff, it was donated after being 'rescued' from a skip, possibly during some renovation work that took place many years later, although it is puzzling and somewhat disappointing that such an item could have been discarded. Incidentally, the Boer War Memorial from the drill hall now hangs in the reception area of Runcorn's town hall.

Following the Armistice in November 1918, talk had quickly turned to how the town could mark the victory and commemorate those who had fallen. One suggestion, put forward by local resident Arthur Dodd, who was a personal acquaintance of Todger, was the proposal that Runcorn's memorial should depict Todger Jones. Dodd reasoned that Todger was the perfect representation of the British 'Tommy', in both physical appearance and physique. Dodd's points were of course correct but the idea, although considered as a viable option, was not acted upon, and in 1920 when Runcorn's war memorial was unveiled, it bore no mention of, and held no link to Todger. This decision was undoubtedly correct. The memorial is a shrine of remembrance dedicated to the fallen, and having a local hero immortalised on it could only serve to deflect attention from what is the sole focus of the monument: to remember those who gave their lives.

It would take ninety-six long years, but Alfred Dodd's suggestion would finally come to fruition. In 2014, a bronze statue by award-winning sculptor David Annand was installed in Runcorn opposite the town's war memorial. The land in which the statue was installed was donated by Robert Harold Posnett to the people of Runcorn after the war to act as a memorial garden where the public, particularly those who had lost loved ones, could sit in contemplation and reflect on the conflict and the huge loss of life that Runcorn had sustained. Its location, facing the memorial, was perfect.

Robert Posnett was the owner of the Camden and Highfield Tanneries, JP, and chairman of the Runcorn Urban District Council. As well as the memorial garden, he owned the land upon which the town's war memorial was erected. He resided at 'The Mound', an impressive house close to the war memorial and garden. He was a hugely important figure in Runcorn's history, and his generosity in giving away his land for the good of the town stretched far and wide and included the donation of three large fields—gifted to the council on the understanding that they would not be built on and would remain as parks or play areas for the town's children.

The statue of Todger Jones serves two purposes. This was made clear by Tony Miller, the founder of the statue appeal who emphasised the importance of the double meaning from the outset of the project. Primarily, it is a statue representing Runcorn's 'favourite son', but its other purpose is equally as important and would undoubtedly have met with Todger's personal approval.

Throughout his life, Todger was quick to deflect any praise away from himself, choosing instead to highlight the contributions of others who were fighting. In one interview with a local reporter, it was recorded that Todger 'was terribly reluctant to speak of himself' and that he spoke of 'every other lad out there' doing his bit without gaining glory.[4]

In life, Todger represented those others who were fighting with his words of support for their plight. Now, as explained on the information board situated alongside the statue, he also represents them in death:

> Thomas 'Todger' Jones was an ordinary working class Runcorn man who performed an extra-ordinary act of valour. However, Todger's statue is much more than a tribute to the man himself. His background is typical of the majority who make up our armed forces. This also makes him the perfect representation of those order ordinary men and women who have served on land, sea or in the air on behalf of the country, and who are equally deserving of recognition by the community for whom they served, or continue to serve.
>
> Todger's statue stands within the Memorial Garden, bequeathed as a place of contemplation and remembrance for the families of those who died, originally in the Great War but also in following conflicts.
>
> Similarly, the statue also stands alongside the Cenotaph Memorial where the names of those who have fallen in service over the decades are enshrined. The location is then the historical focal point for the town's remembrance of our armed forces personnel who never returned home. Like his contemporaries on the Cenotaph, Todger served his country, endured the privations and stresses of active service but unlike them was one of the fortunate ones that returned home. He survived the lottery of battle in that terrible Great War where many of his contemporaries died and so it is appropriate that his figure now stands within sight of their commemoration and acts to ensure we remember not only those we lost in battle but their living comrades to whom we are also indebted.
>
> As is common across the country, Runcorn has no dedicated commemoration to show appreciation for those who served and survived or continue to serve and will eventually return to our community. These service men and women blend quietly back into civic life, many bearing the weight of physical and mental injury without complaint. More unfortunate is that with their eventual passing and as memories fade into the fog of time, the part they played as individuals tends to be lost as society moves on, more concerned with the here and now of its own time and space.
>
> It has always been difficult to acknowledge the debt owed to the unsung many due to the variety of armed services and periods of history involved. It required

> an appropriate common symbol to represent the ethos of their commitment, which had not been forthcoming. However, in the character of Todger Jones and through his statue we now have a personification that reflects those faceless many that served unrecognised. Todger may have served in the army but he nevertheless came from the same stolid stock that also populated and continues to populate not only the Army but also the Royal Navy and the Royal Air Force.
>
> We therefore hope that you, dear visitor, look upon this statue of Thomas 'Todger' Jones not just as a tribute to one man's incredible bravery and personal achievement on the battlefield, but more importantly in the wider context of being an average service man. He stands as testament to all those former and presently serving personnel who receive no individual honour as did Todger, but whose contribution as members of our armed forces and society deserves not to be ignored or forgotten.[5]

On 25 September 2016, as part of a government initiative to mark the centenary of Great War VCs, a paving stone installed in front of Todger's statue was unveiled by Runcorn's mayor and Todger's great nephew Percy Dunbavand, while the author of this book provided a speech describing Todger's exploits.

Maj.-Gen. (ret'd) Skempton (the former CO of the Cheshire Regiment) and various local dignitaries, the Cheshire Regiment Association and other armed forces groups, and members of the general public attended the event.

Other forms of remembrance include a blue plaque that was installed on a small surviving segment of Princess Street—the remainder having been demolished in the early 1960s. Another plaque, unveiled in 2000, is mounted on the outer wall of the old police station on Bridge Street, Runcorn, which is now used by Halton Community Partner Trust. The modest unveiling was attended by the mayor and mayoress of Halton, Joe Darlington, and Percy Dunbavand, with Norman Neale as flag bearer.

Additionally, an illuminated scroll was presented to Todger by the Urban District Council. It is now in possession of Halton Council. In Runcorn, there is a Morval Crescent, named as such after the Battle of Morval in which Todger earned his VC, and there is no mistaking the origins of a more recently developed road in Runcorn, called 'Thomas Jones Way'.

A memorial to Todger and Halton's two other VC recipients—Thomas Mottershead VC, DCM, and Thomas Wilkinson VC—is situated in the grounds of Halton British Legion in Runcorn and an identical memorial is also located in Widnes' Victoria Park, the town where the other two Thomases resided. There is also a memorial tablet installed on the floor of the regimental chapel in Chester Cathedral in honour of Todger, and the regiment museum, also in Chester, houses a number of items relating to him. These include the majority of his medals, his bullet-holed helmet, a pocket watch, and the Iron Cross, 'liberated' by Todger from the Prussian Guards officer that he had killed in a hand-to-hand contest after it had conveniently fallen from his advisories pocket.

Other items have found their way into private collections, and two engraved shell casings adorned with details of Todger Jones appeared on *The Antiques Roadshow* a number of years ago.

In Runcorn, the Todger Jones VC Cup is awarded annually to the winner of the Runcorn Darts League. The Todger Jones Memorial Cup is also awarded on a yearly basis after being reintroduced in 1997 after a lengthy hiatus, with the Runcorn and Halton branches of the Royal British Legion competing for the cup.

17

In His Own Words (and Other Accounts)

The following account from a sergeant stretcher-bearer, 'who saw the incident from start to finish', featured in the *Runcorn Guardian* on 3 November 1916. The article was titled 'How Jones Won the V.C.—An Eye-Witness' Amazing Story':

> What I want you to know about happened on 25th September, when we took a village. We had advanced rather too quickly and won our objective 20 minutes before time. We started to dig ourselves in as quickly as possible. We were not digging many minutes before bullets began to fly. Jones turned to his officer and said: 'They nearly got me, come on, let's go and get without them. There will be trouble for us if we don't'. The officer declined to let him go, and told him to go on digging. We got to work again, and soon two or three bullets whipped past Todger's head. A moment later a chap standing against him got one in the leg. He turned to the officer and said 'If I've got to be killed I'll be killed fighting, not digging'.
>
> Off he went 'on his own'. The lads thought it was the last of him, as our barrage was very heavy on the place he was going to. We watched every second expecting to see him go down, until he jumped into the trench. Some said: 'Poor old man'. They saw the enemy jumping about and thought they had got him. Seven or eight minutes afterwards two more of his chums came up, and when they heard what had happened they said: 'If "Todger" is over there we are going for him'. Two more joined them, and they went across. This is what they found:–
>
> There was 'Todger' standing by 100 of the enemy in a big hollow. He was ordering them to put on their coats. With his pals he rounded them up and brought back over a hundred, including a general staff officer.

Splendid Bravery

> After a while we got out of him a little of what happened. As he went over a bullet went through his helmet and three through his coat, but he took no notice. When he got to the trench he got three of them straight away, and started to settle them as he met them. They bolted into their dug out and commenced to pop at him from the doorway. He got all of them that tried to get him. He flung a bomb down the nearest dug-out, and three came running out with their hands up. Todger asked if any spoke English, and on said he could, so he told them they could either be taken prisoner or be killed. He added that he would prefer to kill them! He told one of the Germans to tell his mates to come out of the dugout one at a time and any man who came out with arms would be shot. They came out, and when his chums came across they said it was the finest sight they had ever seen. I tell you there was a shout went up when Todger led his 100 prisoners into our lines.
>
> Eleven officers recommended him for the Victoria Cross. He is 'top hole'. He has earned it many a time, but has been unlucky in that the people who count were not there at the time.

This account from Sgt Tugg, RAMC, was published in the *Western Gazette* on 10 November 1916 under the header: 'How "Todger" Jones Won his V.C.—Single-Handed Capture of 102 Huns':

> Sergeant Tugg states that on September 25th, after British troops had taken a village and started to dig themselves in, bullets began to fly all round. Jones turned to his officer and said, 'They nearly got me, let's get at them, or there will be trouble'.
>
> The officer declined to sanction the charge, and the shower of bullets continued, a man next to Jones being hit.
>
> Jones said to his officer, 'If I'm going to be killed, I'll be killed fighting, not digging'. He grabbed his rifle and walked over to the German trenches alone.
>
> 'Everyone expected him to go down instantly, and we learned later that one bullet had gone through his helmet and three through his tunic. We gave him up when we entered the German trench, but eight minutes later two of his pals said, "He's gone and we're going, too."' Others followed, and when they got across they saw a sight they'll never forget.
>
> 'There was Todger Jones standing by a hundred of the enemy in a big hollow. He was threatening them with bombs, and they all had their hands upheld. He told them to put on their coats and his pals helped to round them up.'
>
> 'They included a German Staff officer. From the prisoners Jones' comrades learned that he had bombarded the door of their dug-out.'

'One by one they came out and lined up until 102 stood before the dauntless bomb-thrower.'

Sergeant Tugg adds that the men in the trenches went almost wild when Jones returned at the head of his captives, and 11 officers joined in recommending him for the V.C.

An article from the *Illustrated London News*, 17 April 1948:

How many Englishmen to-day, I wonder, remember 'Todger' Jones? It is nearly thirty-two years since this remarkable Englishman and inveterate humorist carried out his greatest jest which won him the Victoria Cross.

It occurred on September 25, 1916, when the 1st Cheshires, during the prolonged battle of the Somme, captured the village of Morval and the ridge on which it stands. As the great prospect that opened up over the German back-areas became visible from the summit, the spirits of the attackers rose, and Private Thomas Alfred Jones whose popularity among his comrades was at this time based on his fame as a humorist in camp and billet, was inspired by the occasion to perpetrate a joke which no Englishman has equalled since the days of Drake's exploits on the Spanish Main.

Without a word to anyone, he took occasion of a lull in the fighting—for the battalion had taken all its objectives—to leave the ranks and set off on his own account in the direction of the enemy lines. Shortly afterwards he encountered a sniper, who tried to kill him, but, being an exceedingly fine marksman, it was he who killed the sniper. He then proceeded, rifle in hand, on his way, stalking and potting a couple more snipers as he advanced. After a time—for he was now moving far in advance of the British Army and had passed through the main German lines—he came to an enemy reserve-trench honey-combed with deep dug—outs. No-one appeared to be at home, but Private Jones, who, like a true Cheshire man, went little by appearances, put his ears to the ground and listened. Soon, as he expected, he heard the sound of guttural voiced conversing under the earth. To these he at once joined his own homely accents, bidding those below to come out and lay down their arms without further ado. This, aware that one who brooked no denial was outside, they obediently did, to the tune of a score or so.

Having lined them up and laconically covered them with his rifle, this worthy Englishman proceeded to the next dug-out, where, in the manner of Captain Hook summoning Peter Pan's hideout under the ground, he again called on the Teutons within to come up and out and join his trail of captives.

When he had emptied half a dozen dug-outs in this methodical way, he counted his bag and, finding now that he had more than a hundred Germans on his hands, including several officers, turned them about and set of for home as though it was all the most natural thing in the world, marching them, to their alarm, through the British protective barrage. Such was 'Todger' Jones's great jest and such the exploit for which he received the country's supreme award for valour and—the first of all rewards to a true humourist—the delighted enjoyment of his comrades. I hope the Homeric tale of 'Todger's' doings that day is still told in his old regiment and that he will be honoured there, in the place where such a man would most wish to be honoured, so long as the regiment endures, and that that will be till the end of time. For so long as the Cheshire Regiment endures, two things will certainly also endure—courage and humour; two of the few really good things to be found on this corrupt, cruel, and rather unsatisfactory planet.

An article published in the *Yorkshire Evening Post* on 10 November 1916:

A Town's Welcome to V.C. Who Caught 102 Germans.
'Todger' Jones describes his Daring Exploit.

'Todger' Jones, the private of the Cheshire Regiment, who won the Victoria Cross by capturing and disarming, single-handed, 102 Germans, and marching them as prisoners to the British lines through a heavy artillery barrage, has arrived at Runcorn, on a visit to his parents. It was a glorious home-coming—a reception worthy of the hero's exploits.

As soon as the news came that he was travelling by the afternoon train from Euston spread, the schools and works declared a half-holiday. In two hours streets were thronged, shops and houses were decorated with flags, and the hero alighted from the train to the accompaniment of enthusiastic cheering and music of brass bands. He embraced septuagenarian parents and brothers and sisters on the platform, and was carried shoulder-high part of the way home, accompanied by the chairman and vice-chairman of the local Council.

In Devonshire Street, the principal thoroughfare, progress was impossible, and finally Jones took to his heels down a side street to his home, arriving almost exhausted. Later he addressed the crowd from a bedroom window, calling for three cheers for the lads still in the trenches, and for the wounded soldiers from the local hospital, who had formed a guard of honour for him at the station.

Describing his arrival at the end of the enemy trench from which he began his marvellous 'round up,' he said he encountered three Germans. 'But I soon got without them,' he added, smiling. 'I happen to be a good shot.'

As he made his way along the trench, with bullets whizzing past him, he met other Germans, who looked militant, and 'got without them' also—with his gun. Presently another batch of the enemy came running towards him holding their hands up, and he took them prisoners.

'I said to one of them,' he continued, 'Can any of you chaps speak English?' and one of them replied, 'I can.' Then I said: 'Now, what has it got to be? You must either be taken as my prisoners or be killed. I'm not particular myself.' The English-speaking chap replied, 'There are a lot more of us here'; but I said, 'I don't care for those; what's it going to be?' and he said, 'I think we will be prisoners.'

Jones then sent the man who could speak English to each dug-out in turn which numbers of the enemy were assembled with the message that if they would surrender their lives would be spared, but that they must leave their equipment behind them. They streamed out of their dug-outs until more than a hundred stood submissively before the solitary Englishman.

One German Who Tried to Escape

'There were so many of 'em that I didn't know what to do with 'em at first,' said Jones, 'but I sent them to get their greatcoats to be going on with. They all started off at once, but I said, 'Here, half a mo'; only two at a time, if you please.'

'One tried to escape, and bolted across a potato field. The potatoes were pink kidneys—I saw them because our shells were digging them up. I put a bullet through the bolting German's head, and he fell and turned over like a rabbit. Then all the others put their hands up. I could not help laughing.'

'How did I feel all this time?' 'Oh, quite cool and cheerful!' 'When you've made the first plunge you feel you can go on for ever doing that sort of thing.'

The *Runcorn Weekly News* published the following article in November 1916, shortly after Todger had returned home from the front. Poxon is incorrectly named as 'Bogson' in the original text, but is amended here for consistency:

Private Jones' Wonderful Narrative
'Up went the hands and I laughed like blazes'

In an interview with a representative of the Weekly News last evening, Private Jones told a very graphic story of the feat which won for him the highest distinction to be gained on the field of battle. The incident occurred on the 25th September, when orders were given to take a certain village. They succeeded in this and had got to the edge of a wood outside the village where they were commanded to dig in and consolidate the position. They were engaged in digging themselves in when bullets commenced flying around. 'They are going to make it hot for us if we don't reach their position,' observed Jones to his officer. 'No,' said the officer. 'We can't go for them yet, you get on with your digging.' 'I said, "All right" and we went on digging,' said Jones.

'The bullets again came flying round, and some of the chaps behind waiting their turn to take the pick and shovel were hit. I looked over the parapet and saw what appeared to be like a white flag. That put the wind in me and I said, "See that sir?", and he said, "Yes," and a few more words. I said, "What do you think of that?, let's go and get them." But he would not allow us, saying he dare not leave that place. "All right," I said, "If I have to be killed I'll die fighting not digging." With that I jumped up and went across and while I was going one bullet went through my steel helmet and four through the side of my tunic. I made for the end of the trench, I remembered my bombing training and that by approaching that way only one at a time can deal with you. Well, three of them came along and I soon put them out and I had my magazine going fairly. Anyhow, they must have had enough, for others behind bolted back into their dug out'.

'For a minute or two they kept coming to the door of the dug out and having a pop at me, but I was a bit lucky, I suppose. I picked up a bomb and threw it into the dug out and three chaps came out holding their arms up and calling out "Kamerad." I shouted, "What's it going to be? Do you want taking prisoner?" One man who could speak English said, "Yes." I asked him how many were down there, and he replied, "about 15." I said, "Ask them if they want to be taken prisoner. My mates are coming across and if they find anything wrong with me they will cut you to bits." He went back, and on returning said they were all willing to be made prisoners. I said that anyone who came up with arms or equipment would get shot straight away. I said, "Get them out of their dug-out" and that was when the procession started.' He, Private Jones laughed heartily at his recollection of the incident. 'They came tumbling out of their dug outs, and I should think there were about eight or nine dug outs altogether. When I got them all lined up I wondered how on earth I was going to get them out of it, and I stood looking at them for a bit. I thought some of my mates would be coming in a bit. That is the way with British troops, they won't leave you in a tight corner alone, and we expected another regiment to come up and relieve us any time. To put on the time a bit I told the chap who could speak English that it was very cold where they were going that night and they would take their greatcoats, and I told them to fetch them two at a time. They kept going in twos for their mantles, as they call them, and this kept things going for eight or nine minutes.'

'There was one big fellow I did not like the look of, and when he went for his mantel I kept half an eye on him. When he got to his dug out about 50 yards he made a dash. I whipped around and with a lucky shot made a sieve of him and he rolled over like a rabbit. "Any more of you want to escape?" I turned round and asked the others, but up they swung their hands until I laughed like blazes. I told them to put them down, but they would keep them up. I turned to have a look over the top, and saw some of our chaps coming across, one of them being my best mate, Poxon, and three others. I can tell you my heart went up with a jump when I saw them, and when Poxon came over he say: "Hello Todger, what the ----- are you doing?" and slapped me across the earhole. Anyhow they helped me to round them up, 150 of them, including a General Staff Officer.'

'I suppose the lads raised a yell when they saw you he was asked. "Yell, you should have heard it,"' and here Private Jones broke off to speak in the highest possible praise of Poxon. 'That chap has deserved recognition hundreds of times. He is a stretcher-bearer, and goes out after wounded many and many a time, and has carried scores of wounded lads in. He risks his life over and over again to save others lads. He deserves something. It's a shame he has not had it before now. He's as brave a fellow as there is in the army. When he knew I had gone across he said: "I'm going after Todger wherever he is, and I'll bring him back alive or dead." I tell you it was grand to see him. When we got them across the officer made me take the prisoners down the line about four or five miles. I was wounded in the shoulder at the time and that made me worse.'

'"I suppose you have been recommended by a number of officers" was our representative's enquiry. "Yes" was the reply. There were line regiments on each side of us, and the officers were able to see through their glasses what was going on. They afterwards sent up to find the name of the man who had done it.' How Private Jones came to hear of the honour having been conferred on him has its amusing side, showing how little Private Jones estimated what was certainly a most marvellous performance, probably one of the most remarkable in the whole history of the war. 'How I got to know of it?' said Private Jones in response to a question. 'Well I had completely forgotten it when a chap came to me and said, "Have you a Victoria Cross?" I said, "No, but I've an Iron Cross here if you're trading."' This Iron Cross, by the way was one Private Jones had picked up, having seen it roll from the pocket of an officer of high rank as he fell, and evidently only just been awarded. Proceeding with his story, he continued: '"Well," said the chap, "No I don't mean that. It's quite right." "What are you getting at?" I asked. "Are you potty, hop it my lad," and I left him. I was then met by a Sergeant, who said, "Put it there, my lad," holding out his hand. "Look here," I said, "What's up with you all this morning?" and he replied, "It's all right my lad, I am right glad to shake hands with you." Well, I went to the transport Sergeant and asked if there was any mail and he came over to me and said, "Put it there young fellow, and the best of look with you," holding out his hand. "Look here," I said, "Will you tell me what's the matter with you all this morning, I don't know what you're getting at," and for an answer he handed me a telegram from the depot at Chester congratulating me. I knew there was something up. "Hearty congratulations from all ranks at the depot, Chester," was the substance of the telegram. Then I got a notification from headquarters and I realised what it was.'

'Were you recognised coming through London?' our representative asked. 'No I saw to that' said Private Jones knowingly. 'At Euston, though, the stationmaster recognised me and one or two more wanted to know if they could do anything for me.' 'I suppose you were surprised at the crowds at

Runcorn?' he was asked. 'What, not half. If I'd known there was going to be such an affair I should have gone round some other way. I'd almost as soon go back to where I came from than face it again.' Private Jones spoke of some of the engagements in which he and his regiment had taken part in and said they had succeeded where other regiments had failed. He had seen German bodies piled high in front of their lines, and even seen British and German dead lying clutching each others throats or each with their bayonets through the bodies of their opponents.

That the V.C hero has more than a passing thought for the comrades he has left behind is shown in the appeal made on behalf of the lads of the original expeditionary force, There were not many of them left, he says, and they have been through two winters in the trenches and stood the brunt of Kaiser Bill's first mad rush. He makes an appeal for these lads to be enabled to have a good rest, for they thoroughly deserve it. It was a pity to see them day after day, week after week, and month after month still pegging at it without any hope of a real good rest and change. For these lads he asks that arrangement should be made for their replacement by other men who have not yet seen the front, and if he were able to carry back good news of this kind he would be almost as pleased as if he were to win further distinction on the battlefield.

The following highly detailed account was originally published in 1917 (*True Stories of the Great War Vol. IV*). Edited sections of the narrative have featured in several places since then, including *The Poona Star* on 24 August 1929, which focused solely on the VC act.

It is published here in its entirety.

Todger Jones, V.C.

The Man Who Captured a Hundred Germans
Single-Handed

His Story as Told by Himself, set down by A. E. Littler

'How the dickens did you do it, Jones?' asked King George, when he invested Private Jones with the well-earned Cross, and out readers will echo the question. Here is the answer—Todger's own modest account of his amazing feat, as told to our representative at a special interview. It is a story that will live, a record of dauntless pluck and unfailing cheerfulness in the face of death that has no parallel even in the glorious annals of the Victoria Cross. Told by *Wide World Magazine*.

I–'Todger' Jones Tells His Tale

'If I've got to be killed, I'll die fighting, not digging.' It was with these words on his lips that Private 'Todger' Jones leaped from the British trenches.

This is the spirit of the soldier who killed several Boches, and by a wondrous piece of bluff, combined with consummate valour, took no fewer than a hundred and two Germans as prisoners. One of the most highly-placed men in London has described it as 'the doughtiest deed of the war', and the description is fully merited.

It was with the object of obtaining the story first-hand from Private Jones's own lips that the writer visited the little Cheshire town of Runcorn, a place proud of its historic traditions, but prouder still of Jones V.C.

Brown-eyed, lithe, clean-cut, and on the slim side is 'Todger', keenly intelligent, with a streak of fatalism in his composition that has sustained him through untold trials, modest as the true hero always is, humorously tolerant of the worship he is commanding, lavish in praise of his comrades yet reluctant to speak of himself.

'Surely,' said he, when approached afterwards, 'there has been "nuff said", more than enough of a thing that was done on the spur of the moment by a man who kept his head and knew how to use his gun. But if you want to know what I did, let the official account speak for me.'

And 'Todger' handed the cold, matter-of-fact narrative set forth in the *London Gazette* as follows:–

> The Victoria Cross has been conferred upon Private Thomas Alfred Jones (11000), Cheshire Regiment, for most conspicuous bravery. He was with his company consolidating the defences in front of a village, and, noticing an enemy sniper at two hundred yards distance, he went out, and, though one bullet went through his helmet and another through his coat, he returned the sniper's fire and killed him. He then saw two more of the enemy firing at him, although displaying a white flag. Both of these he shot. On reaching the enemy trench he found four occupied dug-outs and, single-handed, disarmed one hundred and two of the enemy, including three or four officers, and marched them back to our lines through a heavy barrage. He had been warned of the misuse of the white flag by the enemy, but insisted on going out after them.

'Won't that fit the bill?' observed Jones, but when told that our readers wanted the story in full, and that it ought to be set down for the benefit of posterity, he resigned himself with a sigh. Then, with a smile like a benediction, he spoke as follows:–

It was on September 25th that we took a village that I am forbidden to mention by name, and were just beginning to dig ourselves in near the wood when bullets commenced to whiz past us, wounding one of our men in the head and making things decidedly uncomfortable. I felt the bullets ping-pinging by me and I said to the officer, 'they're going to make it hot for us, Sir, if we don't get after 'em. Can I get out and have a packet at them?'

'My orders are to consolidate this position,' replied the officer. 'You must not go an inch farther, and you had better get on with your digging.'

And dig I did, but as I got up again I saw a chap hit through the head and another through the thigh. Looking ahead, I saw what appeared to be a white flag, and that fairly riled me. My dander was up and I shouted to the officer, 'What do you think of that Sir?'

'You must get on with your digging, Jones,' said he; but up I jumped and called out, 'If I've got to be killed, I'll die fighting, not digging.'

I waited no longer, but dragged out my rifle, flung down my entrenching tool, jumped out of the trench and went across. The Huns were a couple of hundred yards away and they could see me coming. One bullet went 'sss' through my steel helmet and four more through my jacket. There was a sniper in a tree but I soon counted him out. On I went and reached a 'bay', or traverse, leading to the German trench. There were three men in it, but jumping in at the end of the trench, I had only one at a time to deal with. I got my back to the wall, and they whipped round on me. I always believe in firing from the hip and very quickly number one dropped dead. Before the next man could recover his senses I had shot him as well, slipped another cartridge in the breech and got the old magazine going on the third at a yard range. The other man fired at me from the entrance to the dug-outs, but I managed to 'get there' first every time, which is a great thing in jobs of that kind. In the second traverse there were five chaps standing behind one another. One of them made for me with his bayonet, but I bowled him over like the others by the old trick of shooting from the hip.

II–How the Germans Surrendered

I got the five of them, and some of them made awful noises, screaming and squealing. I stalked through the trench, storming and shouting, and, hearing the firing and the commotion, the rest of the crowd bolted in the dug-outs. Soon they had all 'gone to earth' and I was there alone. When they got into their dug-outs I had them where I wanted them. It was just as if you were in a coal-cellar and I was in the street waiting to pot you as you came up. They were shouting and screeching, and every time I saw a movement I let fly.

Eventually, they quieted down, and seeing some of their bombs, a pile of them, on the floor of the trench, I picked up a couple and sent them flying down the first dug-out and they went off all right. I think they felt that the game was up when the bombs began to drop amongst them, for out rushed three fine specimens with their hands up and the usual cry 'Mercy, *Kamarad*!' They had left equipment behind them to show there was no 'monkeying' and though I felt like laughing at being there all on my own, I demanded in a stern voice if any one of them could speak English.

One of them called out 'I can.'

'Well,' said I, 'what's it to be? Do you want to be killed or taken prisoners? You can have it either way you like, for I am not particular. In fact, I would rather kill you.'

And all with one consent actually cried out that they wanted to become prisoners and with Private Jones as their jailer, too!

I looked round and saw a hollow, so I told the English speaking German to order his two mates to get in there. They had to climb up to do it, and I knew our chaps would see them from our trench as they got on top.

'How many more are there down the dug-out?' I asked, and the Boche answered 'about fifteen.'

'What about it?' I said, and he replied 'what do you mean?'

'Do they want killing or what?' said I, and he gasped, 'I don't know.'

'You know they're no use?' I said, and he replied, 'Yes, they're helpless now.'

'Well then,' said I, 'go and tell them what I have told you—that they can be killed or taken prisoners, and they can bloomin' well please themselves about it.'

And, by gum! He went and told them and came back to say they would all be taken prisoners.

'Well then,' said I, 'tell them they can come out when you call, but only one at a time, remember, and any one of 'em that has as much as a penknife on him, or any equipment, will be shot dead straight away. Fetch 'em up one at a time and tell them that my mates are coming across in thousands in a couple of minutes and if they find anything wrong with me, they'll cut you to bits.'

I heard him yowling down the dug-outs what I had told him, and, meanwhile, I got round the cover. Presently he came back and said 'are you ready?' 'Yes,' I replied 'call them up, and only one at a time and no rushing.' He shouted the message and ordered them out without equipment. There were eight or nine dug-outs in all and they kept tumbling out and as they came I sent them out of the trench into the hollow I've told you of.

Lord! I'd expected fifteen and out they came in scores and went in my 'compound.' When they were all out, I threw some of their own bombs into the dug-outs to make sure that there was no sniper left behind to 'do me in.' And then I said to myself 'Great Scot! What am I going to do with this little lot?' I knew I could eventually rely upon somebody coming from our trenches, but it was necessary to gain time.

It's not that I want to brag, but I didn't turn a hair; I just kept my head-piece going. I told them it would be a very cold night at the place where they were going to, and suggested they had better get their great-coats. I graciously permitted them to fetch them—'two at a time, and no rushing.' They ran and came in and out, and each time they passed me they saluted me—Private Jones!—and I sent them to their places. I didn't like the look of one 'bloke' and kept half an eye on him. 'I think I'll shoot that chap,' I said to the interpreter.

'Don't,' he exclaimed, 'he very good man.' But presently the 'very good man' went for his great-coat and when he had got a short distance he made a dash for liberty. I swung round, clicked my rifle and got him fair and square. He rolled over and over just like a rabbit. It was a snap-shot, but I put one through his head. Then I turned to the German by me. 'Ask them if any more would like to try to escape,' I said. He did so, and they all jumped up—they were seated on the ground—flinging up their arms and shouted '*Kamarad*!'

III–'Hand's Up!' I Couldn't Stop Bagging Germans

It fairly tickled me to death that did and I couldn't stop laughing. Why? ... I once saw at a pantomime flashed through my mind. A comedian who played the part of the squire, revolver in hand, rounded up all the servants, male and female, butlers and gardeners, and up went their hands. Then he came to the grandfather clock, pointed his revolver at it, shouting, 'Hands up!' and immediately the hands of the clock whizzed round.

Well, I tell you I roared with laughter at the thought coming into my mind at such a time, when I was playing a lone hand, for it looked so comical to see them all with their hands up—over a hundred of 'em—hoping against hope that Private Jones, *Kamarad*, wouldn't shoot.

I wondered what was going to happen next, for it was out of the question that one chap could keep them there for any length of time. But the bowling over of the chap who tried to escape was the best thing that could have happened to me and it fairly put the fear of God into the rest. The official report speaks of me bringing in a hundred and two, but though I didn't check their numbers, there must have been nearly and hundred and fifty of them when I got them into the open including four or five officers and any number of non-coms, or whatever the Germans call them. But before they got into our lines, over forty of them were killed by our shells, which were sweeping the ground and clearing things up generally.

But I'm over-running my story. I had scarcely finished laughing at the clock putting its hands up, when I saw somebody start from our lines. It was my chum coming to look for me. He had been asking where I was and when they told him, he said: 'If Todger's across there, I'm going to fetch him, dead or alive!' They all though I was a 'goner,' but, when they saw my chum start, three more chaps—a sergeant-major, a corporal and stretcher bearer—came across with him. Seeing I was alive, my chum gave me a smack on the face and couldn't stop larking.

They helped me to 'round up' the 'bag' and we marched them back to our lines. All the time our guns were knocking the position to bits and, as I've said, some of the shells dropped amongst the prisoners and killed them. I got a shrapnel wound in the neck from our barrage, but it wasn't much. Strictly speaking, I suppose I ought never to have been in the game, but I wouldn't have missed it for the worlds. When I went over my arm was a bit painful, for I was wounded on September 5th, and had refused to go into hospital.

Looking back and thinking over the incident, I feel that I must have had what the poets call 'a charmed life,' for, after jumping out of the trench and before I had accounted for the sniper in the tree, a bullet went through my helmet and was buzzing round my head-piece like a marble in a basis, finally galloping down my back and burning me during the journey. Four or five other bullets passed through my tunic, but I wasn't aware of it until afterwards. It never entered my mind that I should be killed and I didn't think my time had come.

Asked if he could explain how he was led into the exploit 'Todger' said, with a grin, 'when I saw the first three men in the bay I knew I was up against something, but I had been in more than one tight corner before and I had learned that the art of warfare–for the individual, as any rate, was to size up a situation quickly, to fire without hesitation and hit your man'

'And,' inquired the interviewer, 'was there no period during the incident that you felt that the proposition was too big for you?'

'I should be lying,' was the answer, 'if I didn't admit that I was glad, jolly glad, to see my pals come over, but I was cool as cool could be, and the lesson I applied was never to lose this (significantly touching his head). The man who loses his "nob" is done for. I knew if I had to go I should, for everybody has his time, that's what I believe and I meant to sell myself at a good price. But when I got the first men in the traverse and drove the others back into the dug-outs, I felt that the game was in my hands. I had them at my mercy; they didn't know I was unsupported; I cowed them into submission to my orders; I pictured the end that awaited them if a hair of my sacred head was singed, and my trump card was played in making them come out one by one without any equipment.'

IV Jones Tells Another Story

Pressed—and it should be understood that the man whose deed Sir Frederick Norman has described as 'big stuff' was terribly reluctant to speak of himself—pressed to recount some other vivid experiences which have been hinted at, Private Jones was compelled to admit that on two or three other occasions prior to the capture of the hundred and two Germans he had been promised special mention, but the officers who had noted him were killed before the opportunity of recommending him for honours arose.

'It isn't every heroic deed that is noticed,' said the soldier. 'Many's the chap who earns the V.C. who never gets a 'Thank You.' Every lad out there is winning, though not receiving, glory; they are brave, noble, clean-fighting, staunch and true men, and if they haven't had my luck they've deserved it.

'But if you want to now what further part I have played in the war, and my preparation for the big slaughter, I may say I was an old Volunteer of the Cheshire Battalion, and that the skill I acquired as a marksman sixteen or seventeen years ago led me to being employed at the Front as a sniper and bomb-thrower. By trade I am a fitter, and am thirty-six years of age, and I tried to join the Engineers at the outbreak of war, but as a Territorial Reservist was eventually posted to the Cheshire Regiment, and found myself at the Front in January, 1915.

'Amongst the narrow shaves I have had may be included a bullet through my pouch, the heel of my boot blown away, and an explosion of a shell which lifted me ten yards in the air and lodged a piece of shrapnel in my shoulder and another piece in my knee.

'Hill 60 was one of my hottest trials, and there I had my first experience—second hand, fortunately—of the German poison-gas. We had only been relieved the night before, and wanted a rest badly, but at ten o'clock in the morning we received word that something had happened at Hill 60, and it was up to us to try to set it right. We got through Ypres town to the railway cutting, and there came under heavy shell fire. Bad wasn't the word for it, for they were bowling the lads over right and left, and as we got closer and closer their machine-gun fire was mowing us down something cruel.

'Eventually we took cover in the railway cutting and met the Germans coming along four deep. We received orders to charge, and cleared them off the railway line, and then we had to start with the trenches. No sooner had Colonel Scott given the word, as he stood by my side, than he dropped mortally wounded. We didn't wait for further orders, for we saw red, and cleared the second line of trenches. Then we made another charge, and took the original trench, which had been held by the Dorsets.

'There they sat, staring at us. "Matey, you've relieved," we said to one, but there was no answer. "There's some hot tea waiting for you in Ypres," we said to another. No answer. They were dead–gassed, and we didn't know then of the diabolical device that had killed them. I was one of forty-three who went out that night to bomb the Germans, expecting that another regiment would take over the trenches from which we had driven the enemy.

'We used up all our bombs, and the Germans began to bomb us in turn. Our lieutenant was the only man with a revolver, and he used it until he had no more ammunition left and was shot. All except three of us and a corporal were either killed or wounded, and the corporal asked me if I could lead them back. I did it, and reported to the company officer, who said he had received reports on which he was going to recommend me for honours. A brave officer—reported from that very day as missing, as was the lieutenant.

'We also went through the battle of St. Eloi, which lasted three weeks. We were at Hill 60 when it was blown up, and we remained in the trenches for twenty days, and after just one night out put in another forty-three days, which constitutes a record either in the French or British Army for continual fire-trench work. We were even reduced to the necessity of sewing sandbags together to serve as a change of 'linen.' When the hill went up it was a sight one can never forget, while the shelling of Ypres was more like a mighty firework display than anything else.'

V–How I Got the Iron Cross

'The first trenches I was in were only thirty-five yards from the Huns. We caught a squad of them working in the rear of their trench. We soon downed them, but the others spotted us, and rattled at us for forty-eight hours. We dared not show our heads above the trench, but I was acting as guide, and one night I turned out to look for an N.C.O. who had been sent with a message and had failed to return. He had had to go through two woods in the dark, and I made sure he had lost his way. I took the turn he would have done had he gone wrong, and after going about two thousand yards I stepped through a gap in the hedge and got a nice little shock.

'Lying on the ground about a yard from me were three Huns with helmets, rifles. And full kit! I whipped my rifle from my shoulder and butt-ended it, meaning to make a good fight for it. I noticed they did not move, so I stepped closer in, and saw the frost on their packs. Then I knew they were dead.

'My first thought was souvenirs. I got in between the dead men, and was going to begin collecting, when a star-shell went up, and I soon found I had landed between our own lines and the Germans. They spotted me, opened rapid fire, and sent up light after light. I flung myself into a ditch and waited about ten minutes. I don't know how I escaped being hit, for the bullets struck all around me. All thoughts of souvenirs had gone out of my head. When they ceased I made a sprint for it. I did 'even time' that night, and was mighty glad when I found the missing N.C.O.

'At another place we had a very rough time of it. Hell seemed to be let loose, for shells were dropping into our trenches, mortars blew the bags down, we were under rapid fire from the German trenches, and to cap the game they had mined the trench and tried to blow it up, but they had gone too deep, and only one or two of our lads were buried, and were safely dug out again.'

Side by side on the table Private Jones placed his V.C. and a silver-edged German Cross of the 'second degree,' one the very embodiment of modest worth, the other blatantly arrogant.

'And yet,' said Todger, 'looking upon the two emblems, and then turning his eyes upon a large official photograph of himself and his flock of a hundred and two Huns, and anon taking in at the glance of a gold watch, a silver teapot, an illuminated address, and other public tributes to his valour—'and yet, next to the V.C., I think more of that Iron Cross than all of the rest, and God knows how much I appreciate all that my fellow-towns-men have done for me.

'But it's quite another story,' he protested, when asked for an explanation. 'I won that Cross in a single-handed joust with a company commander of the First Prussian Guards. And I don't think he had chance to wear it! But he had to go, for there was only him and me for it, and I didn't see why Jones should be turned down.

'The fact is, it was the last scrap I was in before I won the V.C., and it was there that I got wounded in the shoulder. I don't think there's any harm in telling you it was at Guillemont–Mouquet Farm and the stronghold around. The Germans had beaten back all attempts to take it from them. Division after division had tried to wrest it from them and had failed.

'Then they brought up our division, and once again we were told that we had been called out to do what others had failed to do. It was a terrific struggle, and we were repulsed four times. Our company had to take the lead at the fifth charge. The bombers won through and leapt into the trench.

'We knocked the machine-gunners over and helped the following waves to get through with little loss. It was a terrible journey—the worst, I believe, that I have been through.

'Yes, I'm coming to the Iron Cross by degrees. I had a wild three minutes, a rare good do. We got rid of those about us, and I rushed into the next traverse and met my man, a fine big chap, full of fight, a commander of the swell crowd, the First Prussian Guards.

'He made for me with bayonet, but I knew too many tricks even for a Prussian Guard, and I soon settled him. The Iron Cross, in its little case, fell from his inside pocket as he dropped. It's new; I suppose he'd just received it from the Kaiser. Poor beggar! I'll never forget him when I look upon the Cross I won from him in a fair fight.

'We were then reinforced, and advanced another three thousand yards past Guillemont and dug in, being too exhausted to go any farther. We stayed there until relieved in the early morning, when we went into support about six hundred yards behind, and the shelling was very heavy. It was here I got wounded. It happened in this way.

'A party was lost, and I told them I would take them down for a drink, as they had been without food and water for over sixty hours. I got them to the place they had to stay at, got the water, and was making back when one of the big shells plumped alongside me and lifted me about ten yards, a piece getting me in the right shoulder and leg.

'I refused to go down the line, and though my arm was useless for a day or two, and was a bit stiff and painful when I won the V.C., it was all a streak of luck, for if I'd gone to hospital I should have missed the funniest round-up I've ever seen.'

VI–'It Was Just My Luck.'

And with this Private Jones was brought back to his starting-point. He simply blushed when reference was made by the interviewer to some of the things that have been said and some of the eulogies passed upon his prowess. He admitted that he was filled with pride when he was ushered into the presence of the King to receive his decoration. 'I was a bit flustered at first,' said 'Todger,' 'but His Majesty made me at home. One of the first things he said to me when the record was read was, "How the dickens did you do it, Jones ?" I won't tell you what I answered on the spur of the moment, but the King laughed, and so did I. "It was just my luck," I said to His Majesty. "I was like a man with his back against the wall, and I kept my head," And then I gave him an idea how the thing had been done, and he laughed at the thought of me fetching home my happy little family."

Throughout the recital Private Jones made no secret of the fact that his nickname is 'Todger.'

'Why 'Todger'?' I inquired, and the V.C. man chuckled just as one may imagine he chuckled when he remembered the pantomimic hold-up.

'I was afraid you'd come round to that,' said he, 'but there it is, and there's no getting away from it. I was 'Todger' at school, and 'Todger' followed me to France. It's like this. As a boy at school I played football, and I suppose I was a bit tricky or artful when it came to dribbling. My school-fellows nicknamed me 'Dodger,' but my front name is Tom, and it wasn't long before it was 'Todger' this and 'Todger' that. It was 'Todger' with everybody at the Front, and lots of 'em seemed to know me by no other name.'

Runcorn feels itself honoured by Jones's wonderful prowess. Thousands of people met him upon his return, a marble tablet is to record his deeds. His employers have provided his parents with an annuity of fifty pounds per year, he has received a gold watch, an illuminated address, framed photographs, a smoker's cabinet, a silver wrist-watch, a silver teapot, a case of cutlery, field-glasses, and a host of other things. He has also had a civic reception at Chester, been entertained at dinner by the Cheshire Regiment, chaired round the Castle square, and been photographed and filmed.

APPENDIX I

Hugh Colvin VC

Just two men of the Cheshire Regiment have earned the VC, and both were for actions in the First World War. The second of the regiment's VCs was awarded to 2Lt Hugh Colvin of the 9th Battalion. It was gazetted on 6 November 1917 with the following citation:

> When all the officers in his company except himself—and all but one in the leading company—had become casualties and losses were heavy, he assumed command of both companies and led them forward under heavy machine-gun fire with great dash and success. He saw the battalion on his right held up by machine-gun fire, and led his platoon to their assistance. Second-Lieut. Colvin then went on with only two men to a dug-out. Leaving the men on top, he entered it alone and brought up 14 prisoners. He then proceeded with his two men to another dug-out which had been holding up the attack by rifle and machine-gun fire and bombs. This he reached, and, killing or making prisoners of the crew, captured the machine-gun. Being then attacked from another dug-out by 15 of the enemy under an officer, one of his men was killed and the other wounded. Seizing a rifle he shot five of the enemy, and, using another as a shield, he forced most of the survivors to surrender. This officer cleared several other dug-outs alone or with one man, taking about 50 prisoners in all. Later he consolidated his position with great skill, and personally wired his front under heavy close range, sniping in broad daylight, when all others had failed to do so. The complete success of the attack in this part of the line was mainly due to Second-Lieut Colvin's leadership and courage.[1]

Hugh Colvin was born on 1 February 1887 at Rosegrove, Burnley. He enlisted in the army in September 1908 as a private in the 8th (Royal Irish) Hussars. He was serving in India on the outbreak of the war.

On 13 April 1917, he was commissioned as a second-lieutenant and posted to the 9th Battalion, Cheshire Regiment, where he was soon carving out a reputation as a gallant officer. He earned a divisional commendation in June 1917 for his daring reconnaissance and patrol work in the Messines area when he 'mopped up' a number of enemy dugouts that were hidden and hitherto unknown.

Colvin received his VC at the hand of the king at Buckingham Palace on 28 November 1917, after which he received a civic reception at Chester, during which he spoke in a similar manner to Todger Jones by speaking of 'the brave men who had earned the Victoria Cross "by the bucketful", only to be killed with their deeds unwitnessed'.[2]

Post-war, Colvin continued to serve in the regiment. He retired as a captain in 1935 and went on to serve as an army recruitment officer (1938–45) before settling down in Northern Ireland. He died in Bangor, County Down, on 16 September 1962 and is buried in Carmoney Cemetery, near Belfast.

APPENDIX II

Todger's Siblings

Joseph Edward Jones (1868–1923)

Joseph was employed as a construction worker in a local chemical works. In 1890, he married Annie Molyneux (1872–1931). They lived at 27 Egerton Street in Runcorn and together had six children: Annie Lilian Jones (1890–1970); Joseph Edward Jones (1893–1962), whose service in the Australian Army during the First World War all but destroyed him; Thomas Clifford Jones (1894); Sarah Maud Jones (1897); Charles Leonard Jones (1906–26); and Mary Beatrice Jones (1911), who is the mother of Anne Bamber, whose recollections feature earlier in this book.

Emma Jones (1870–1956)—Known as Emily

Throughout her life, Emma was known as Emily to her friends and family. In 1890, she married David Lightfoot (1867–1947), who was employed as a chemical labourer and later a 'pipe fitter'. They lived at 51 Princess Street and had four children: Charles Edward Lightfoot (1891–1961); Frank Leonard Lightfoot (1893–1964); George Frederick Lightfoot (1897); and Florence Elizabeth Lightfoot (1901).

Frederick Jones (1873–1925)

In 1894, Frederick, who worked as a chemical labourer, married Mary Elizabeth Caldwell (1874–1901) and together they had a son, Peter Caldwell Jones (1894–1962). In 1904, three years after the death of his wife, Mary, Frederic married

Elizabeth Louisa Thornton (1882–1951). By 1911, they were living at 6 Princess Street. Together they had five children: Ivy Elizabeth Jones (1904–97); Charles Edward Jones (1907–95); George Frederick Jones (1909–85); Lilian Jones (1911); and Emily Jones (1914–87).

Peter Jones (1875–1926)

Peter was a steward at the Widnes Branch of the Liberal Club. Little is known of his life.

Lilly Jones (1878–79)

Charles Arthur Jones (1884–1917)

Charles was known as Arthur to his friends and family. As described earlier in this book, he served as a private in the 10th Battalion, Cheshire Regiment (Regiment No. 15088). He was discharged from the Army in June 1916 after being shot in the head by a sniper on 6 October 1915. He died at home on 30 July 1917.

Sarah Maude Jones (born 1887)

Sarah married Richard H. Williams in 1915, but little else in known of her life.

Walter Jones (1890-1937)

In 1911, Walter was an apprentice boiler maker. In 1915, he married Hilda Bayes (1891–1958) in 1915. They had a daughter, Gladys Jones, who was born in 1917.

APPENDIX III

Todger's Funeral

The following list of names was published in the *Runcorn Weekly News* on 10 February 1956 as attending Todger's funeral:

> Chief mourners:—Mrs E. Lightfoot (Sister), Mr & Mrs W. Turton (Sister & Brother in Law), Mrs Hilda Jones (Sister in Law), Miss Gladys Jones (Niece), Mrs Annie Pearson (Niece, of Newton Le Willows), Mr & Mrs C. E. Lightfoot (Nephew & Niece), Mr & Mrs Fred Lightfoot (Nephew & Niece), Miss Joan Lightfoot (Great Niece), Mrs F. Anderton & Mr T. Anderton (Niece & Nephew), Mrs Lucy [this was Ivy, not Lucy], Dunbavand (Niece), Mr Alan Rose (Great Nephew), Mrs Traida & Mr Sam Walker (Great Niece & Nephew), Mrs Clara & Mr Jack Fearnett, Mrs Jenny & Mr Sam Fryer (Cousins).
>
> Among the general mourners were:–Mr F Richardson, Mr D McDermott, Mr P Davies (Parish School). Mrs MacGregor, Mr W MacGregor, Mr G Thompson, Mr R Hallwood, Mr E Hancock, Mr P Kelly.
>
> The Cheshire Regiment was represented by Colonel Hayes Newington OBE (representing Brigadier General Brodie CB, OBE, DSO, Colonel of the 22nd Cheshire Regiment). Representing the 4th Battalion, Major J. H. Sharpley OBE (also representing Brigadier General G. P. Harding OBE, OBE, MC), Major J. H. McGuiness (also representing Lieutenant Colonel J. W. Cotterell OBE), Major A. P. Trueman & Captain A. L. Hayes Newington. Representing the 7th Battalion, Major G. O. Thompson, Captain J. R. Billington, Lieutenant W. M. Cobb, R.S.M. F. Turner, R.S.M. O. A. Frazer, R.S.M. W. H. Day, Colonel F. L. Abel, Major R. Osborne MBE, MM, MSM (representing Colonel A. R. Crookenden), Major P. Andrews. Depot at Chester, Lieutenant A. F. W. Astle, 2nd Lieutenant F. J. Goddard, Bugler, Drummers, Williamson and Gittens.
>
> Among the British Legion representatives were C. L. Cohen (Pres, Runcorn Branch), David Hazlehurst (Chairman, Runcorn Branch), Mr J. Teasdale (Pres,

Weston & Weston Point Branch), Mr J. Pugh (Chairman, W & Weston Point Branch). There were also representatives from Chester, and members of the Ladies Sections of Runcorn and Weston & Weston Point.

Wreaths were sent by Sister Em, Sister Maud & Billy, Sister in Law Hilda and Gladys, Niece Annie & Family (N le W), Nephew Charles, Elizabeth and Joan, Nephew Frank and Leonard, Nephew Fred and Bertha, Niece Florrie and Tom, Nephew Peter and Family, Bootle, Nephews Charlie and George, Ivy and George, Niece Emily, Eddie and Family, Niece Betty and Alan, Niece Traida and Sam, Niece Dorothy and Arthur (New Market), Cousins Clara & Jack (Port Sunlight), Cousin Rev. F. Massey, Doris and Ellen (Australia), Cousin Jenny and Sam (Stockham Lane), Members of the Cheshire Regiment Association, and many friends.

Endnotes

Introduction

1 *True Stories of the Great War Vol. IV* (acknowledged and republished from *Wide World*). Also published in *The Poona Star*, c. 1929.

2 Martin-Leake's VC was announced in *The London Gazette*, 13 May 1902. He was a Surgeon-Major with the South African Constabulary at the time:

> During the action at Vlakfontein, on 8th February, 1902, Surgeon-Captain Martin Leake went up to a wounded man, and attended to him under a heavy fire from about 40 Boers at 100 yards range. He then went to the assistance of a wounded Officer, and, whilst trying to place him in a comfortable position, was shot three times, but would not give in till he rolled over thoroughly exhausted. All the eight men at this point were wounded, and while they lying on the veldt, Surgeon-Captain Martin-Leake refused water till every one else had been served.

Leake's bar featured in *The London Gazette*, 16 February 1915, with the following citation:

> For most conspicuous bravery and devotion to duty throughout the campaign, especially during the period 29th October to 8th November 1914, 1914, near Zonnebeke, in rescuing, whilst exposed to constant fire, a large number of the wounded who were lying close to the enemy's trenches.

3 The third man to be awarded the VC and bar is the New Zealander, Captain Charles Upham. These were awarded for actions during the Second World War.

4 Lister's VC citation was announced in *The London Gazette*, 23 November 1917:

> On 9 October 1917 east of Ypres, Belgium, seeing that the advance of his company was held up by machine-gun fire from the direction of a pillbox, Sergeant Lister dashed ahead of his men and found the gun—he shot two of the gunners and the remainder surrendered. He then went to the pillbox and shouted to the occupants to surrender. They did so with the exception of one man whom the sergeant shot,

whereupon about 100 of the enemy emerged from the shell-holes further to the rear and surrendered.

5 See, for example, *The Oak Tree Journal*, and the *Chester Chronicle*, 11 July 1942.
6 Hodgkinson, P., *Glum Heroes*, (Helion Publishing) p. 47 quoting Cuddeford, D. W. J., *And All for What*, London, Heath Cranton, 1933.
7 *Illustrated London News*, 17 April 1948.
8 *Cheshire Observer*, 28 August 1954 (Todger made this comment during the 1954 Mons Day reunion).

Chapter 1

1 Fanny's father—Todger's maternal grandfather—was Peter Lawson (*c*. 1818–95), who was a labourer. Peter's wife was Martha Lawson (*c*. 1806–83). As well as Fanny, the couple had three other children; James Lawson (*c*. 1834), Thomas Lawson (*c*. 1836), and Peter Lawson (*c*. 1839).
Edward and Fanny's children were John Jones (*c*. 1837–77), William Jones (*c*. 1840), Edward Jones (*c*. 1843), Thomas Jones (*c*. 1844), Joseph Jones (*c*. 1848), and Henry Jones (*c*. 1854). The family lived in Nelson Street, Runcorn.
2 Joseph Edward Jones (1868–1923), Emma Jones (1870-1956), Frederic Jones (1873–1925), Peter Jones (1875–1926), Lilly Jones (1878–79), Thomas Alfred Jones (1880–1956), Charles Arthur Jones (1884–1917), Sarah Maude Jones (born *c*. 1887), Walter Jones (1890–1937). Note: for fuller details refer to Appendix I.
3 The school has since been demolished and a replacement—the All Saints CE Primary School—built nearby.
4 In 1908, upon the formation of the Territorial Force, the medal had replaced the Volunteer Long Service Medal that had previously been issued for long service. In 1920, the Territorial Force became known as the Territorial Army and the medal that Todger had received was replaced by the Territorial Efficiency Medal.

Chapter 2

1 Zuckerman, L., *The Rape of* Belgium (New York: New York University Press, 2004).
2 It should be noted that supporting primary source material of this is lacking. Therefore, authentication of this widely-believed occurrence is decidedly difficult to confirm.
3 Sometimes referred to as the Battle of Miani.
4 Brigade Structure:

1st Battalion, Norfolk Regiment
1st Battalion, Bedfordshire Regiment (left the brigade on 1 November 1918)
1st Battalion, Cheshire Regiment
1st Battalion, Dorsetshire Regiment (left the brigade in November 1915)
1/6th Battalion, Cheshire Regiment (joined brigade 17 December 1914 and left it on 1 March 1915)
1/6th (Rifle) Battalion, King's Liverpool Regiment (joined brigade 27 February 1915 and left on 18 November 1915)
16th (Service) Battalion, Royal Warwickshire Regiment (joined brigade 26 December 1915, and left on 4 October 1918)

15th Machine Gun Company, Machine Gun Corps (formed 27 December, and moved to 5th Battalion Machine Gun Corps 26 April 1918)
15th Trench Mortar Battery (formed April 1916)

5 This message is reproduced in *The Cheshire Regiment and its Miniature Colour at Mons*, by F. Simpson.
6 *Ibid.*
7 *Ibid.*
8 WO95/1571, 1st Battalion, Cheshire Regiment, War Diary.
9 In an article from 31 January 1956, following the death of Todger, the *Birmingham Daily Post* stated, 'he joined the First Battalion Cheshire Regiment on August 5th, 1914, being the second man to be enlisted at Runcorn Drill Hall at the start of the war'. However, an article in the *Nantwich Guardian* states that he was the fourth man.
10 8534 Pte George Dunning. Home address given at time of enlistment was 33 Fryer Street, Runcorn. Date of Death: 19.10.14. 7451: Pte Joseph Jones was born in Runcorn and enlisted in Chester. He was thirty years old at the time of his death and was the brother of Mrs Martha Ann Grimes, of 6 Norton Street, Runcorn.
11 *Ever Glorious: The Story of the 22nd (Cheshire) Regiment, Volume I—1689–1939* (Chester: kmcreative, 2002).
12 Crookenden, Col. A., *The History of the Cheshire Regiment in the Great War* (1938).
13 Hussey, Brig.-Gen. A. H., and Inman, Maj. D. S., *The Fifth Division in the Great War* (London: Nisbet & Co. Ltd, 1921). See also, Crookenden. *op. cit.*
14 Crookenden, *op. cit.*
15 *Runcorn Guardian*, 9 April 1915.
16 *Ibid.*
17 *Ibid.*
18 Undated extract from a letter by Private Newton, 1st Cheshire Regiment.
19 *Runcorn Guardian, op. cit.*

Chapter 3

1 The 22 April was the first time that chlorine gas had been used, but it was not the first time that gas in the wider sense had been deployed as a weapon. Tear gas had been used by both the French and Germans prior to this, although the effect on those in its path had been minimal.
2 WO95/1571, 1st Battalion, Cheshire Regiment, War Diary.
3 *History of the Dorsetshire Regiment 1914-1919* (Uckfield: Naval Military Press Ltd, 2002) reprint.
4 *Ibid.*
5 *Ibid.*
6 Crookenden, Col. A., *The History of the Cheshire Regiment in the Great War* (1938).
7 Greg, A., *The Oak Tree*, *c.* 1915. Greg's account was later republished in the regiment history.
8 *Ibid.*
9 Miller, F. T., (editor-in-chief), *True Stories of the Great War Volume IV* (New York: Review of Review Company, 1917).
10 *Ibid.*
11 *Ibid.*

12 *Ibid.*
13 WO95/1571, 1st Battalion, Cheshire Regiment, War Diary.
14 *Ibid.*

Chapter 4

1 *The Oak Tree, 1924.* Note: Greg's account was later republished in the regiment history: Crookenden, Col. A., *The History of the Cheshire Regiment in the Great War* (1938).
2 *Ibid.*
3 *Ibid.*
4 Miller, F. T., (editor-in-chief), *True Stories of the Great War Volume IV* (New York: Review of Review Company, 1917).
5 *The Oak Tree*, and Crookenden, Col. A., Arthur Greg account, *op. cit.*
6 *Ibid.*
7 *Ibid.*
8 *Ibid.*
9 *Ibid.*
10 Gillon, Capt. S., *The K.O.S.B. in the Great* War (London: Thomas Nelson & Sons Limited, 1930).
11 Hussey, Brig.-Gen. A. H., and Inman, Maj. D. S., *The Fifth Division in the Great War* (London: Nisbet & Co. Ltd, 1921).
12 *The Oak Tree*, and Crookenden, Col. A., Arthur Greg account *op. cit.*
13 *Ibid.*
14 *Ibid.*
15 *Ibid.*
16 Lt Arthur Greg died on the same day he was wounded (23 April 1917). He is buried in the north-east quarter of Jussy Communal Cemetery. His observer, 21451 Air Mechanic 1st Class Robert Robson, died on 18 May, aged twenty-one. He is buried in the Bois-Guillaume Communal Cemetery Extension. Interestingly, Herman Göring is believed to have been flying one of the enemy machines that took part in the dogfight. Göring went on to command the Luftwaffe (German air force) in the Second World War, and became one of Germany's highest-ranking officers.
17 *Cheshire Observer*, 5 May 1917.
18 2Lt Robert Philips Greg died three days after receiving his wounds. He is buried Lijssenthoek Military Cemetery.
19 Miller, F. T., (editor-in-chief), *True Stories of the Great War Volume IV* (New York: Review of Review Company, 1917).
20 *Ibid.*
21 WO95/1571, 1st Battalion, Cheshire Regiment, War Diary.
22 Hussey, Brig.-Gen. A. H., and Inman, Maj. D. S., *op. cit.*

Chapter 5

1 Crookenden, Col. A., *The History of the Cheshire Regiment in the Great War* (1938).
2 Macdonald, L., *They Called it Passchendaele* (London: Penguin Books, 1993) reprint.
3 Howard Marten, a conscientious objector, *c.* 1974.

4 WO95/2243, 10th Battalion Cheshire Regiment War Diary.
5 *Ibid.*
6 125612 (PO) William Walter Allaby, aged forty-seven. HMS *Velox*, Royal Navy. Son of John and Sarah Ann Allaby. Born in Aston, Cheshire.
7 During his presentation speech, William said he 'had assisted in rescues at sea, and hoped he would always be fit and ready to do so again if the occasion arose.' He is buried in Runcorn Cemetery.
8 Hussey, Brig.-Gen. A. H., and Inman, Maj. D. S., *The Fifth Division in the Great War* (London: Nisbet & Co. Ltd, 1921).
9 The 9th Battalion were also involved, albeit not in the actual attack. They were ordered to move forward to reinforce troops of the 34th Division in a captured German line, setting off on the 1st, and arriving in the early hours of the following morning.
10 *Runcorn Weekly News*, *c.* 1916.
11 Crowdy, T., (editor)m *Donald Dean VC* (Barnsley: Pen & Sword, 2010).
12 *Ibid.*
13 Ainslie, Maj. G. M., *Hand Grenades: A Handbook on Rifle and Hand Grenades*, 1917.
14 WO95/1571, 1st Battalion, Cheshire Regiment, War Diary.
15 *Ibid.*
16 *Ibid.*
17 *Ibid.*
18 *Ibid.*
19 Miller, F. T., (editor-in-chief), *True Stories of the Great War Volume IV* (New York: Review of Review Company, 1917).
20 DSO announced in *London Gazette*, 20 October 1916. Allan Gwynne-Jones was a prolific artist, teaching at the Royal College of Art where he became a professor of painting (1923–30). He then joined the staff of Slade School of Fine Art. In 1980, two year before his death, he was appointed Commander of the Order of the British Empire (CBE).
21 Miller, F. T., (editor-in-chief), *op. cit.*
22 *Ibid.*
23 *Ibid.*

Chapter 6

1 WO95/1571, 1st Battalion, Cheshire Regiment, War Diary.
2 Hussey, Brig.-Gen. A. H., and Inman, Maj. D. S., *The Fifth Division in the Great War* (London: Nisbet & Co. Ltd, 1921).
3 One such source, *I Laughed Like Blazes*, p. 13, states 'He [Todger] had just witnessed the shooting of 18-year old runner Pte George Kenworthy who had been killed whilst digging next to him'.
4 *Cheshire Observer*, 28 August 1954.
5 10026 Pte Kenworthy, from Oldham in Lancashire, entered France in October 1914. He spent time as a convalescence patient in Rouen before joining up with the battalion at the end of March. His military career was rather colourful. He was awarded fourteen days' field punishment (No. 1) on 2 May. This was followed by a further twenty-eight days' FP No. 1 for misconduct was issued to him on Christmas Eve and he had four days' pay forfeited. In June 1916, he again committed misconduct, which resulted in another seven days of the lesser FP No. 2.

6. Miller, F. T., (editor-in-chief), *True Stories of the Great War Volume IV* (New York: Review of Review Company, 1917).
7. *Ibid.*
8. *Runcorn Guardian*, 3 November 1916.
9. *Ibid.*
10. Miller, F. T., (editor-in-chief), *op. cit.*
11. *Ibid.*
12. *Ibid.*
13. *Ibid.*
14. *Ibid.*
15. *Ibid.*
16. *Ibid.*
17. *Ibid.*
18. *Ibid.*
19. *Ibid.*
20. *Ibid.*
21. *Ibid.*
22. *Chester Chronicle*, 11 November 1916.
23. Miller, F. T., (editor-in-chief), *op. cit.*
24. WO95/1571, *op. cit.*
25. *Ibid.*
26. *Ibid.*
27. Hussey, Brig.-Gen. A. H., and Inman, Maj. D. S., *op. cit.*

Chapter 7

1 *Runcorn Weekly News, c.* 1916.
2 *Runcorn Weekly News, c.* November 1916 and *Manchester Evening News*, 27 October 1916.
3 *Ibid.*
4 *Ibid.*
5 *Runcorn Guardian*, 27 October 1916.
6 *Ibid.*
7 *Runcorn Guardian*, 3 November 1916.
8 *The Oak Tree*, November 1916.
9 *Runcorn Weekly News*, 3 November 1916.
10 1308: Pte L. Pollit. Notification of his DCM was published in *The London Gazette*, 30 June 1915 with the following citation:

For conspicuous gallantry during the night of 24th March 1915, when he assisted in bringing into safety a Non Commissioned Officer & two men who were lying in the open under fire.

11 *Runcorn Guardian*, 10 November 1916.
12 *Chester Chronicle*, 11 November 1916.
13 *Ibid.*
14 *Ibid.*
15 *Runcorn Guardian*, 10 November 1916.
16 *Runcorn Weekly News*, 10 November 1916.
17 *Runcorn Guardian*, 10 November 1916.
18 *Ibid.*

19 *Ibid.*
20 *Ibid.*
21 *Ibid.*
22 *Ibid.*
23 *Ibid.*
24 *Ibid.*
25 *Ibid.*
26 *Ibid.*
27 *Ibid.*
28 *Ibid.*
29 *Ibid.*
30 *Ibid.*
31 *Hull Daily Mail,* 11 November 1916.
32 *Chester Chronicle*, 11 November 1916.

Chapter 8

1 *Stoke Sentinel*, 8 September 2014.
2 Records show that Todger arrived on 16 January and Poxon on the 19th.
3 Lucy, J. F., *There's a Devil in the Drum* (Uckfield: Naval Military Press, 2009).
4 Poxon 'left the trench' on 25 February 1915 while the battalion was in reserve at Dranoutre.
5 WO95/1571, 1st Battalion, Cheshire Regiment, War Diary.
6 *Stoke Sentinel*, *op. cit.*
7 *London Gazette,* 16 November 1916.
8 As was eluded to in the *Stoke Sentinel, op. cit.*
9 *Stoke Sentinel, op. cit.*
10 *Runcorn Weekly News*, 3 November 1916.
11 *Chester Chronicle,* 10 November 1916.
12 Miller, F. T., (editor-in-chief), *True Stories of the Great War Volume IV* (New York: Review of Review Company, 1917).
13 Poxon served in the 453rd Company of the Royal Defence Corps. He was a private with the regiment number 69847. Although difficult to decipher, his records also mention something about the 6th Royal Welsh Fusiliers, although it is unclear whether or not he actually served under them. This was during his time at home following his wound.
14 Poxon, British Army service records, 1914–1920.
15 For further information on Class 'P' Reserve use the following link: www.longlongtrail.co.uk/soldiers/a-soldiers-life-1914-1918/enlisting-into-the-army/british-army-reserves-and-reservists/.
16 *Stoke Sentinel*, *op. cit.*
17 *Ibid.*
18 *Ibid.*
19 *Ibid.*

Chapter 9

1 The ranks of these men from the deed to presentation may differ. For example, Coury was promoted to a full lieutenant following the act that earned him his

VC but was recorded as a second-lieutenant in the announcement in *The London Gazette*. Likewise, George Sanders was promoted from corporal to sergeant.

2 *London Gazette*, 26 October 1916.
3 Miller, F. T., (editor-in-chief), *True Stories of the Great War Volume IV* (New York: Review of Review Company, 1917).
4 *Leeds Mercury* on 20 November 1916.
5 *Chester Chronicle*, 25 November 1916.
6 *Liverpool Daily Post*, 21 November, 1916.
7 *Ibid.* Note: Todger division was the 5th, not the 6th.
8 *Ibid.*
9 *Ibid.*
10 *Daily Mail*, 11 November 1916.
11 *Nantwich Guardian*, 17 March 1917.

Chapter 10

1 *Chester Chronicle*, 2 December 1916.
2 *Nantwich Guardian*, 5 December 1916.
3 *Ibid.*
4 *Ibid.*
5 *Ibid.*
6 *Runcorn Guardian*, 17 November 1916.
7 *Nantwich Guardian*, *op. cit.*
8 *Ibid.*
9 *Ibid.*
10 *Ibid.*

Chapter 11

1 Crookenden, Col. A., *The History of the Cheshire Regiment in the Great War* (1938).
2 Letter home, 1 February 1918 (note: a contemporary transcript of this letter erroneously notes the year as 1917).
3 *Ibid.*
4 Ludendorff, E., *Ludendorff's Own Story Vol. I* (New York, Harper & Brothers, 1919).
5 Crookenden, Col. A., *op. cit.*
6 *Ibid.*
7 *Chester Chronicle*, 19 October 1918.
8 *London Gazette*, 5 December 1918.
9 *Cheshire Observer*, 28 August 1954.
10 *Chester Chronicle*, 14 December 1918.
11 *Ibid.*
12 *Ibid.*
13 49149 Pte T. C. Evans's DCM citation as follows:

During the advance N.E. of Gouzeancourt in Sept. 18, owing to severe casualties, he assumed command of a platoon and led them forward under heavy fire. On reaching the objective he took forward a patrol and located a machine-gun.

Chapter 12

1 *Runcorn Guardian*, 2 May 1919.
2 *Ibid.*
3 *Ibid.*
4 Hallwood, 1/5th South Lancs, DCM citation:

> For conspicuous gallantry, energy and devotion to duty near Le Touquet from 25th February to 9th April 1915, when engaged in working underground (continually in water) preparing a mine, which was successfully exploded on the latter date. This work was very arduous and most hazardous, as the possibility of the German counter-mine being exploded at any moment was ever present.

5 Medical record show that Joseph was admitted to the 3rd Auxillary Hospital on 20 November 1916 and describe his wounds as to the chest while all other records describe his wounds as to the back.
6 Joseph went AWOL from 3 p.m. on 13 December 1916 until 2 p.m. on 14 December for which he was forfeited two days pay. On 9 February at 2 p.m., he one again went AWOL, this time for a much longer period of seventeen days, until 26 February 1917. For this, he received thirteen days detention after being in custody for three days awaiting trial. He also forfeited four days' pay.

Chapter 13

1 Wheatley, K., *Legacy Vol. 3* (Derbyshire: Spire Graphics Ltd, 2010).
2 *Runcorn Guardian*, 7 May 1915.
3 Lloyd, VC citation, published in *The London Gazette*, 2 January 1894:

> During the attack on the Sima Post by Kachins, on the 6th January last, Surgeon-Major Lloyd on hearing that the Commanding Officer, Captain Morton (who had left the fort to visit a picket about 80 yards distant) was wounded, at once ran out to his assistance under close and heavy fire, accompanied by Subadar Matab Singh. On reaching the wounded officer, Surgeon-Major Lloyd sent Subadar Matab Singh back for further assistance, and remained with Captain Morton till the Subadar returned with five men of the Magwe Battalion of Military Police, when he assisted in carrying Captain Morton back to the fort, where that officer died a few minutes afterwards. The enemy were within ten or fifteen paces keeping up a heavy fire which killed three men of the picket, and also Bugler Purna Singh. The man accompanied Captain Morton from the fort, showed great gallantry in supporting him in his arms when wounded, and was shot while helping to carry him back to the fort. (The Native Officer and five sepoys above alluded to have been awarded the Order of Merit.)

Grimbaldeston, VC citation, published in *The London Gazette*, 14 September 1917:

> On 16 August 1916 1917 at Wijdendrift, Belgium, Company Quartermaster-Sergeant Grimbaldeston noticed that the unit on his left was held up by enemy machine-gun fire from a blockhouse. Arming himself with a rifle and hand grenade he started to crawl towards his objective, and when he had advanced over 100 yards another soldier came forward to give covering support. Although wounded, he pushed on to the blockhouse, threatened the machine-gun teams inside with a

hand grenade and forced them to surrender. The action resulted in the capture of 36 prisoners, six machine-guns and one trench mortar.

4 Hugh Colvin was situated at seat No. 282, Table 10. Pte Christopher Cox VC, and Gunner Charles Stone VC, MM, were seated either side of him.
5 Howard, L., *Thomas Alfred Jones VC, DCM* (Birkenhead: Countryvise Ltd, 2014).
6 *Ibid.*
7 A few people including myself have been informed of this by those connected to the regiment museum over the years. It is also mentioned by Melvin Charles Smith in his book, *Awarded for Valour*, where, he says he was told of the 'dug out' comments on 31 July 1995 during an 'interview with Major (ret) Tony Astle, Acting Regimental Historian of the 22nd (Cheshire) Regiment; as a young officer with the regiment, he knew Jones, and heard a very different version of the deed from the man who did it'.
8 *London Gazette*, 26 October 1916 (VC citation).
9 *Manchester Courier & Lancashire General Advertiser*, 23 September 1914.
10 Bladensburg, KCB, KCVO, Lt-Col. Sir Ross of, *Coldstream Guards 1914–1918* (London: Oxford University Press, 1928).

Chapter 14

1 Paul Smitham (Todger's great-grandson), as described to the author.
2 *Ibid.*
3 *Ibid.*
4 *Ibid.*
5 *Runcorn Weekly News*, 2 September 1927.
6 *Cheshire Observer*, 28 August 1928. Following the publication of this article an interesting letter was received by the *Cheshire Observer* from Jesssie, Annie and Maggie Massey, of 19 St. James Street, Chester. It was published on 4 September 1954:

> Sir.—It was with pleasure we read in the 'Observer' of the visit to The Dale of 'Todger' Jones VC., of Runcorn. We were relieved to know that 'Todger' who is first cousin to my sisters and myself is still alive and well. News we received from several visitors was that he was no longer here. As we have not visited Runcorn for many, many years, we naturally accepted that as true. We were young when 'Todger' won his V.C., but it was a memorable occasion when he was able to visit Chester as the first Cheshire VC of the 1914–18 War. Our parents were both natives of Runcorn, my father being the younger brother of 'Todger's' mother. I, too, was born there, but was brought here to live when a baby, so, of course, consider myself a Cestrian, my younger sisters being born here, too. We would like so much to have seen 'Todger', but thanks to the local press for news of him.

7 As a recipient of the VC, Todger automatically qualified for the Coronation Medals.

Chapter 15

1 *Nantwich Guardian*, 5 December 1916.
2 Todger's records as well as a multitude of other sources (medal roll etc.) show that he was demobilised with the rank of private on 28 May 1919. One such

source was published after his attendance at a reunion where it was stated: 'Mr. Jones entered the Regiment as a private, and left it as a private in 1919' (*Cheshire Observer*, 28 August 1954). Strangely, a *Runcorn Guardian* newspaper article dated 2 May 1919 regarding the Chester parade in which Todger carried the miniature colour, names him as 'Corporal "Todger" Jones'. The following piece also featured in the *Cheshire Observer* many years later on 10 July 1964:

When the padre of the Battalion consisted on 26 men under the command of Capt. (now Major) Sproule M.C., returned from France, they were given a splendid reception on their arrival at Chester on 25th April, 1919. The Regimental Colours were decorated with the oak and acorn wreaths, but the colour which attracted the most attention was the miniature carried by Corporal 'Todger' Jones V.C., D.C.M.

This is not easily explained and may be an error.

3 Richards, F., *Old Soldiers Never Die* (London: Faber & Faber, 1933).
4 *Ibid.*
5 Lucy, J. F., *There's a Devil in the Drum* (Uckfield: Naval & Military Press, [Reprint] 2009).
6 Stone, C., edited by Sheffield, G. D., and Inglis, G. I. S., *From Vimy to the Rhine* (Wiltshire: Crowood Press, 1989).
7 Tucker, J. F., *Johnny Get Your Gun* (Barnsley: Pen & Sword, 2015).
8 Richards, F., *op. cit.*
9 Lucy, J. F., *op. cit.*
10 *Ibid.*
11 *Ibid.*
12 *Ibid.*
13 *Ibid.*
14 Smith, M. C., *Awarded For Valour: A History of the Victoria Cross and the Evolution of British Heroism* (Hampshire: Palgrave Macmillan, 2008).

Chapter 16

1 *Nantwich Guardian*, 5 March 1918.
2 *Ibid.*
3 *Ibid.*
4 Miller, F. T., (editor-in-chief), *True Stories of the Great War Volume IV* (New York: Review of Review Company, 1917).
5 Wording compiled by Neil Thornton and Eric Thornton.

Appendix I

1 *London Gazette*, 6 November 1917.
2 Snelling, S., *Passchendaele 1917, VCs of the First World War* (Stroud: Sutton Publishing Limited, 1998).

Bibliography

Ainslie, Maj. G. M., *Hand Grenades: A Handbook on Rifle and Hand Grenades*, 1917
Atkinson, C. T., *The Devonshire Regiment 1914-1918* (Uckfield: Naval & Military Press, 2001) reprint
Bucher, G., *In the Line 1914–1918* (Uckfield, Naval & Military Press Ltd, 2005) reprinted and translated
Cave, N., *Hill 60: Ypres—Battleground Europe Series* (Barnsley: Leo Cooper, 1998)
Clayton, A., (editor), *Liverpool Heroes Book 4* (2010)
Creagh, O. G., *The Distinguished Service Order 1886–1923* (London: Savannah Publications, 1978) Originally published in 1924; Hayward 1978 reprint
Crookenden, Col. A., *The History of the Cheshire Regiment in the Great War* (1938)
Crowdy, T., (editor), *Donald Dean VC* (Barnsley: Pen & Sword, 2010)
Eden, A., *Another World 1897–1917* (New York: Doubleday & Company, Inc., 1977)
Ever Glorious: The Story of the 22nd (Cheshire) Regiment, Volume I—1689–1939 (Chester: kmcreative, 2002)
Gillon, Capt. S., *The K.O.S.B. in the Great War* (London: Thomas Nelson & Sons Limited, 1930)
Gliddon, G., *The Somme, VCs of the First World War*, (Stroud: Sutton Publishing Limited, 1997)
Hammerton, J. A., *The War Illustrated Album De Luxe Vol. VII* (London: The Amalgamated Press, Limited, 1917)
Hart, P., *1918: A Very British Victory* (London: Weidenfield & Nicolson, 2008)
History of the Dorsetshire Regiment 1914–1919 (Uckfield: Naval Military Press Ltd, 2002) reprint
Hodgkinson, P., *Glum Heroes, Hardship, Fear and Death—Resilience and coping in the British Army on the Western Front 1914–1918* (Solihull: Helion & Company Limited, 2016)
Howard, L., *Thomas Alfred Jones VC, DCM* (Birkenhead: Countryvise Ltd, 2014)
Hussey, Brig.-Gen. A. H., and Inman, Maj. D. S., *The Fifth Division in the Great War* (London: Nisbet & Co. Ltd, 1921)
Lucy, J. F., *There's a Devil in the Drum* (Uckfield: Naval Military Press, 2009)
Ludendorff, E., *Ludendorff's Own Story Vol. I* (New York, Harper & Brothers, 1919)
Macdonald, L., *1915: The Death of Innocence* (London: Penguin Book, 1993); *They Called it Passchendaele* (London: Penguin Books, 1993)

Mace, M., and Grehan, J., *Slaughter on the Some: 1st July 1916* (Barnsley: Pen & Sword, 2016)
Miller, F. T., (editor-in-chief), *True Stories of the Great War Volume IV* (New York: Review of Review Company, 1917)
Oldfield, P., *Victoria Crosses on the Western Front Somme 1916* (Barnsley: Pen & Sword, 2016)
Petre, OBE, F. L., *The History of the Norfolk Regiment 4th August 1914 to 31st December 1918* (Uckfield: Naval & Military Press, 2003; first published Norwich: Jarrold & Sons, Limited, 1924)
Rawson, A., *Loos-Hohenzollern (Battleground Europe series)* (Barnsley: Pen & Sword, 2003)
Richards, F., *Old Soldiers Never Die* (London: Faber & Faber, 1933)
Rogerson, S., *Twelve Days on the Somme, A Memoir of the Trenches, 1916* (London: Greenhill Books, 2006) Reprint; originally published in 1933
Simpson, F. *The Cheshire Regiment OR 22nd Regiment of Foot: The First Battalion at Mons and the Miniature Colour* (W. H. Evans, 1929)
Smith, M. C., *Awarded For Valour: A History of the Victoria Cross and the Evolution of British Heroism* (Hampshire: Palgrave Macmillan, 2008)
Snelling, S., *Passchendaele 1917, VCs of the First World War* (Stroud: Sutton Publishing Limited, 1998)
The 22nd (Cheshire) Regiment, *Ever Glorious; The Story of the 22nd (Cheshire) Regiment, Volume 1—1689–1939* (Chester: kmcreative, 1982)
Thompson, D., *The Parish: The History of Runcorn All Saints CE Primary School* (Widnes: Mailbook Publishing, 2002); *Before Endeavours Fade: The Story of Runcorn in War 1939–1945* (Widnes: Mailbook Publishing, 2003*); I Laughed Like Blazes: The Life of Thomas 'Todger' Jones VC, DCM* (Widnes: Mailbank Publishing, 2002)
Thornton, N., *Led By Lions: MPs and Sons Who Fell in the First World War* (Stroud: Fonthill Media, 2017)
Tucker, J. F., *Johnny Get Your Gun* (Barnsley: Pen & Sword, 2015) reprint
Warrington, P., *For Bravery in the Field: Great War British Army Recipients of the Military Medal 1914–1920* (Uckfield, Naval & Military Press, 2014)
Wheatley, K., *Legacy of the Rorke's Drift Heroes Volume 3*, (Derbyshire: Spire Graphics Limited, 2010)
Zuckerman, L., *The Rape of* Belgium (New York: New York University Press, 2004)

Newspapers, Journals, Magazines, and Websites

Birmingham Daily Post
cheshirecountymemorialroll.com
Cheshire Observer
Chester Chronicle
Commonwealth War Graves
Daily Mirror
Daily Record
Globe
Lancashire General Advertiser
Liverpool Daily Post
Manchester Evening News
Manchester Courier
Nantwich Guardian

Nottingham Evening Post
Portsmouth Evening News
Runcorn Guardian
Runcorn Weekly News
Stoke Sentinel
The Poona Star
Wide World Magazine, *c*. 1917
Widnes Weekly News
The Boys Own Paper
Thegreatwarcheshire.co.uk
The Long Long Trail
The Oak Tree: Journal of the 22nd (Cheshire) Regiment (various editions 1915–1920)
The Leeds Mercury
War diaries (various)
War office papers, including Dunning file, Kenworthy file, Poxon file, Todger Jones file

Index